COOKING UP
THE GOOD LIFE

COOKING UP THE GOOD LIFE

Creative Recipes for the Family Table

Jenny Breen & Susan Thurston

UNIVERSITY OF MINNESOTA PRESS
MINNEAPOLIS • LONDON

Published by the University of Minnesota Press
111 Third Avenue South, Suite 290
Minneapolis, MN 55401-2520
http://www.upress.umn.edu

Library of Congress Cataloging-in-Publication Data
Breen, Jenny.
Cooking up the good life : creative recipes for the family table /
Jenny Breen, Susan Thurston. p. cm.
Includes index.
ISBN 978-0-8166-7566-1 (pbk.)
1. Cooking, American—Midwestern style. 2. Cooking—Middle West.
3. Cookbooks. I. Thurston, Susan. II. Title.
TX715.2.M53B74 2011
641.5977—dc22
2010049105

Printed in the United States of America on acid-free paper

The University of Minnesota is an equal-opportunity educator and employer.

18 17 16 15 14 13 12 11   10 9 8 7 6 5 4 3 2 1

Preface

Jenny Breen

❧

THE FIRST TENDER ASPARAGUS
OF MAY, STEAMED AND DRIZZLED
WITH CITRUS AND BUTTER.

The sweetness of a fresh ear of corn
bursting through the humid swamp of a
July evening. The riot of the rusted palette
of butternut squash, carrots, parsnips, and
beets, caramelized in a bath of balsamic
vinegar and olive oil, eaten on a cool
September night. A bowl of fragrant chowder
thick with potatoes, yams, and leeks to
warm the hands and spirit in the midst of the
coldest December afternoon.

The colors, the flavors, and the pleasure of
eating with the seasons are at the heart of the
Good Life. It is a life where cooking at home
is a joyful experience—for everyone in the
family. In the Good Life kitchen, you will
experience a relaxed approach to creating
wholesome and flavorful dishes that are
simple and quick to prepare, with minimal
fuss and equipment. You will gain an
appreciation for the landscape and soil from
which your food comes, as well as for the
people who work to raise that food. Along
the way, you will save money and minimize
your impact on the environment.

I was born and raised a Jew in Minnesota.
I grew up in an area heavily influenced
by Scandinavian Americans. A strange
combination, perhaps, but a good fit in
many ways. I discovered a like-mindedness
in both ethnicities about the importance
of family, food, and community. The
"Minnesota nice" that surrounded me was
warm and genuine, and my own family's
Jewish obsession with food found its way
into the hearts of our friends.

As long as I have been cooking, I
have experimented with recipes. For me,
developing a recipe is like creating a work of
art. Much of it is spontaneous, unplanned,
unexpected. I often combine things I
have never tried together or go against
common sense to enhance the food's natural
perfection. Through this process I have
come to believe that good cooking is not
about the chef but about the food.

Toward that end, I have constructed
recipes that can be followed over and over
again with the same results, and by different
people. The simplicity of these recipes invites
everyone to be involved with making and
enjoying wholesome and delicious meals. I
have been fortunate to be able to test and
hone these recipes through my teaching at
the Twin Cities Food Co-ops, the University
of Minnesota Landscape Arboretum, and
the College of Continuing Education at
the University of Minnesota. Through
these working relationships I met Susan
Thurston, who said, "Jenny, you should write
a cookbook." To which I replied, "I already
have." Our writing collaboration began at
that point, and she has helped to tell this story.

I believe it is important to learn the story
behind the food you eat. I have been part
of the local and sustainable food movement
for decades, and I am encouraged that many
people now share a basic understanding

of this tradition and practice, and show a growing interest in supporting the farmers and producers committed to earth-friendly growing methods.

Through the recipes in this book, I offer you a distillation of my years of experience in feeding people. You will find easy and delicious recipes to prepare in your own kitchen, confident that they are based on sound nutrition. These recipes were born of my deep passion and ongoing pursuit of the perfect blending of flavor, texture, practicality, variety, and consciousness. My goal is to make this food accessible to everyone, and I hope you will enjoy preparing these foods as much as I have.

Introduction
Jenny Breen and the Good Life
Susan Thurston

YOU ARE A COOK WHO UNDERSTANDS THAT THE STORY BEHIND YOUR FOOD IS AN ESSENTIAL INGREDIENT OF GOOD EATING.

You want to know how and where your food was grown and who was involved in its production. You have a vision of what the good life is, and it has a lot to do with good food. If this describes you, then welcome to the Good Life kitchen, where you learn the joy of linking the pleasures of food and cooking with a commitment to community and the environment. As you nurture yourself and those you love through this approach to cooking, you will improve the health of yourself, your family, and your world.

In *Cooking Up the Good Life*, chef Jenny Breen envisions a kitchen where you, family, and friends share in preparing wholesome and delicious meals. Her recipes feature fresh and simple ingredients. She encourages you to find many of those ingredients at a local co-op or nearby farmers' market, to join a community supported agriculture (CSA) group, or to grow them yourself. She knows that you care about the people who raise that food and the land it comes from—and that you gain deep and satisfying pleasure when the flavors and colors of the season are brought to the family table in delicious and surprising ways.

For Jenny, the Good Life kitchen is at the heart of all she does. When you are in her kitchen, you are with a natural teacher. By following her recipes, which are offered in a refreshingly straightforward style, you will become more confident in making flavorful, unfussy, and elegant meals from whole foods. You can relax knowing that all the ingredients are wholesome and that there is room for spontaneity; go ahead and improvise, make that recipe your own. With Jenny's recipes, you will find ways to include the children in your life while cooking a meal. And ultimately, through nutritious food prepared with joy, we will all feel better about our own health and about contributing to a more sustainable way of living on this planet.

Jenny insists on giving credit where it is due: she joined a rich Minnesota tradition of supporting local and organic growers and farmers. The Minneapolis and St. Paul areas have always been at the vanguard of the local and sustainable food movement. Within a forty-minute drive of either city, farmland surrounds you; on state highways, you need to slow down during planting and harvest for slow-moving tractors and grain trucks.

Farmers and co-ops have held important places in virtually every community in the Twin Cities. North Country Cooperative Grocery (NCC) had the longest run. It was established during the peace and organic food movements in the late 1960s and early 1970s and, after a brief stint on a front porch in the Cedar–Riverside neighborhood, it officially opened its doors in 1971 and rocked people's perceptions of what a cooperative business could be. For many years, it was the soul of that neighborhood and a fixture of Minneapolis. During the thirty-seven years it existed, NCC changed with the times while maintaining its ethic of supplying earth-friendly food to its customers.

A co-op with a more strident political profile was Powderhorn Food Community Co-op. As noted in a history of the co-op compiled by the Minnesota Historical Society, a group of college students started Powderhorn Co-op as a buying club around 1972 and opened a storefront in 1975. During its nineteen years of business, the co-op was a microcosm of the push and pull within the organic and sustainable food movement: some members wanted to focus on providing whole foods to customers, while others who were members of the Co-op Organization (CO) wanted to advance a stronger political agenda on the management. The CO had a central role at other co-ops, including the Beanery Co-op and the People's Warehouse, but at Powderhorn these divisions led to "co-op wars" in the mid-1970s, during which non-CO co-op members broke into Powderhorn Co-op, changed the locks, and installed a new cash register as part of their efforts to alter leadership. Although conflicts were handled with less drama in following years, management and neighborhood changes led to the storefront closing during the winter of 1994.

The Wedge Community Co-op is another co-op with deep-running roots. A familiar feature of its South Minneapolis neighborhood since 1974 (when it was a tiny storefront with vegetables displayed in the cardboard boxes they were delivered in), the Wedge now has more than fourteen thousand members and continues to advance and facilitate ways for customers to keep organic and sustainable food on the table. It became the first certified organic retailer in Minnesota, created a local distribution network with Co-op Partners Warehouse, and purchased the successful Gardens of Eagan, one of the oldest certified organic farms in the Twin Cities area.

While some farmers expanded operations in an attempt to offset a crumbling farming commodities economy, others looked at sustainable and organic farming as a better option. As the economic crises in farming pushed some producers into supersizing their operations, another segment worked to meet an emerging demand for food produced without suspect chemicals and to develop strong local distribution and fair pricing methods. Many of these producers did not emerge from multigenerational family farms, as Gardens of Eagan did, but were instead developed during the 1980s by people who wanted a rural lifestyle. One such farm is Earthen Path Organic Farm (a member of the Full Circle Organic Growers Co-operative), which sells its produce through the Oak Center General Store near Lake City, Minnesota.

During this period, Minnesota took the lead in establishing nonprofit organizations that brought urban and rural residents together to promote sustainable agriculture and stewardship. The Land Stewardship Project is one of the greatest success stories: in 1982 farmers, residents, and public policy makers converged to educate people on the ethics of farmland stewardship and the

CONTENTS

❦ VEGAN   Ⓥ VEGAN OPTION

Creamy Wild Rice Soup ⓥ
Curried Squash Soup ⚘
Winter Fish Chowder
Cashew–Quinoa "Chili" ⚘

Cooking Grains

SPRING
Miso Vegetable Soup ⚘
Spring Greens Soup with Caramelized
  Ramps ⓥ

SUMMER
Carrot–Dill Soup ⓥ
Cold Cucumber–Yogurt Soup ⓥ
Gazpacho ⚘
Borscht ⚘

Early Greens with Miso Dressing and
  Toasted Almonds ⚘
Israeli Couscous

SUMMER
Marinated Veggies ⚘
Potato–Broccoli Salad ⚘
Gingered Green Beans ⚘
Quinoa and Cucumber Salad ⚘
Asian Pesto Rice Noodles with Mock
  Duck ⚘
Fresh Potato and Smoked Salmon Salad
Potato Gratin with Gorgonzola
Southwestern Chicken Salad with
  Cilantro and Orange Dressing

Salads and Sides 57

AUTUMN
New Age Potato Salad ⓥ
Garlic–Almond Kale ⚘
Roasted Roots ⚘
Golden Pecan–Rice Salad ⚘
Luscious Lima Bean Salad ⚘
Quinoa and White Beans with Raspberry
  Dressing ⓥ
Rosemary Chicken Salad

Growing Green Flavor

WINTER
Mediterranean Millet "Couscous" ⓥ
Sesame–Ginger Soba Noodles ⚘
Black Bean, Tofu, and Miso Salad ⚘
Tangy Cashew Wild Rice ⚘

Wild Rice

Herbed Yam and Potato Salad ⓥ
Latin "Couscous" ⚘
Brussels Sprouts with Honey–
  Horseradish Sauce ⓥ

SPRING
Rainbow Rice ⚘
Polenta and Artichoke Salad ⚘
Asparagus and Artichoke Pasta ⓥ
Asparagus with Citrus and Olive
  Marinade ⓥ

Sustenance 89

AUTUMN
Harvest Lasagna ⓥ
Curried Chickpeas and Autumn
  Vegetables ⚘
Shepherd's Pie ⓥ
Autumn Pasta with Tarragon and Cider
  Sauce ⓥ
Polenta with Chicken and Artichoke–
  Tomato Sauce
Pumpkin Ravioli with Corn Cream Sauce
Mediterranean Succotash with Edamame
  and Lime ⓥ

WINTER
African Peanut Stew with Spiced Millet ⚘
Lentil–Walnut Burgers ⓥ
Roasted-Squash Gratin with Cilantro Pesto
Black-Eyed Pea and Sweet Potato Ragout ⚘
Stuffed Squash with Wild Rice, Quinoa,
  and Pine Nut Pilaf ⓥ
Squash–Pecan Croquettes ⚘
Greek Squash or Pumpkin in Phyllo
  Casserole
Turkey and Sheep-Cheese Quiche
Winter Squash and Greens in Coconut
  Milk Curry ⚘
Roasted Winter Vegetable Gratin ⓥ

"*Through the recipes in this book, I offer you a distillation of my years of experience in feeding people. You will find* **EASY AND DELICIOUS RECIPES** *to prepare in your own kitchen, confident that they are based on sound nutrition. These recipes were born of my deep passion and ongoing pursuit of the perfect blending of flavor, texture, practicality, variety, and consciousness.* **MY GOAL IS TO MAKE THIS FOOD ACCESSIBLE TO EVERYONE**, *and I hope you will enjoy preparing these foods as much as I have.*"

importance of creating a farmer-to-farmer network to help farmers achieve more sustainable farming methods and to reduce reliance on factory farming. The Minnesota Farmers' Market Association (MFMA) was created by a group of farmers' markets and advocates to pool resources and wisdom. MFMA fosters community among member markets, facilitates communication and access for communities, and serves as a clarion voice for the common good of new farming groups both to the public and to government.

Clearly, the landscape of farming and food distribution were shifting. During this wave of change, a few cafés and restaurants similarly devoted to earth-friendly ingredients were established. During the 1970s, some were dedicated to vegetarian menus, and all relied on loyal customers from the immediate neighborhood. Some, like the New Riverside Café, become legendary but are no longer operating. Others, like the Seward Café, continue to operate, following cooperative principles and buying from local suppliers.

Jenny came of age during these early decades of the local food movement and soon embarked on a life's calling to cook. She was mentored by and became a part of a unique community of innovative chefs and cooks.

Her first job was at McDonald's. The experience provided a paycheck but also made it glaringly apparent that she wanted to work where people actually cared about the food they prepared and served.

During her junior year of college, Jenny gained an appreciation for the power of the collective while living on a kibbutz in Israel. She worked more than five days a week tending and caring for orchards and gardens that produced abundant food, including avocadoes, almonds, grapes, and jojoba. She became even more determined to create a life where she would braid together her Jewish identity and values, an intimate relationship between food and the body, and a stalwart appreciation of the earth and the sustenance it offers.

After finishing college in St. Louis, Jenny returned to Minnesota. In 1986 she worked at Francesca's, a bakery–café on Selby Avenue in St. Paul. Here the food was homemade, and she expanded her expertise in bread and dessert baking and gained an insider's view of running a small business. Equally important to Jenny, however, was the café's location: just down the street from Francesca's was Café Kardamena, the first restaurant of award-winning chef Brenda Langton. During breaks from cooking at Francesca's, Jenny would take a short walk down the street to stand in the doorway of Café Kardamena and watch, enthralled, as Brenda made her magic. The encounter opened a view of how Jenny wanted to work, although it would be years before she and Brenda would actually meet.

In 1986 Jenny also stumbled on the now-iconic Seward Café. The restaurant, along with several co-ops in Minneapolis, was promoting a small food revolution. The café obtained its mostly organic and all-natural food in bulk from a local cooperative warehouse. For years the Seward Café operated as a collective: there was no single owner, everyone contributed. The food was fresh, organic, and delicious. During her nearly seven years cooking at the Seward, Jenny met local farmers who drove their produce-filled pickup trucks to the kitchen door. These relationships heightened her appreciation for the dishes she would make from what they offered. From Frank Siegle, the mainstay and philosopher at the Seward, Jenny learned even more about the inter- and intra-reliance of people with their food and the history of this movement in the Twin Cities. She learned about preparing whole foods in rhythm with the seasons, and she refined her own food choices and philosophy. She derived infinite pleasure in serving well-made dishes to people who (regardless of their economic backgrounds or their chosen lifestyles) appreciated it. Today the Seward Café is aligned even more closely to organic food sources and purchases its food from numerous local suppliers while also maintaining Hare's Breath Community Garden.

Eventually, it was time to move on. Jenny's energy and ideas were abundant, and the timing was perfect for her and Karn Anderson, a close high school friend from the late 1970s, to reconnect. During Jenny's years at the Seward Café, Karn had managed places such as Kim Bartmann's Café Wyrd in south Minneapolis. Jenny and Karn shared a deep and complex relationship with food, and together they created a small business named Taste Buds Catering. Karn was the front-end representative with customer service savvy and an affinity for table settings; Jenny was involved almost exclusively with the menus and cooking.

During the early 1990s, a number of like-minded cooks and chefs promoted ethical consumerism through their methods and menus. A local food sensibility infused the rich and exuberant flavors brought to the tables of thousands of patrons hungry for this return to the local. Jenny met and connected with other leaders of the local food movement. Through their work with the Youth Farm and Market Project, Jenny met Lucia Watson, the award-winning chef and owner of Lucia's in Minneapolis, and Brenda Langton, her inspiration. Tracy Singleton, another high school friend of Jenny's, was running the Birchwood Café, a similar business.

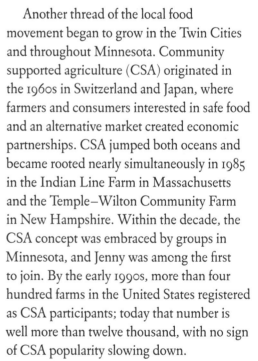

Another thread of the local food movement began to grow in the Twin Cities and throughout Minnesota. Community supported agriculture (CSA) originated in the 1960s in Switzerland and Japan, where farmers and consumers interested in safe food and an alternative market created economic partnerships. CSA jumped both oceans and became rooted nearly simultaneously in 1985 in the Indian Line Farm in Massachusetts and the Temple–Wilton Community Farm in New Hampshire. Within the decade, the CSA concept was embraced by groups in Minnesota, and Jenny was among the first to join. By the early 1990s, more than four hundred farms in the United States registered as CSA participants; today that number is well more than twelve thousand, with no sign of CSA popularity slowing down.

During this time of growth, Jenny

began to teach. Friends and contacts who subscribed to CSAs turned to her for help in learning what to do when, for example, their bushel baskets of produce seemed to contain mostly kohlrabi. Many classes were taught in the Seward Café kitchen, the very place where Jenny had begun exploring the rich options of sustainable foods.

The success of Taste Buds led to a search for a more visible home for the business. In the winter of 1996, the Good Life Café was born. The name was inspired by the book *Living the Good Life* by Helen and Scott Nearing, and Jenny and Karn attempted to reflect the Nearings' ability to manifest their politics and their passion in every aspect of their lives. After the launch of the Good Life Café, Jenny shifted her focus toward recipe creation and culinary teaching. In the winter of 2001, the café was sold free of debt, and the more adaptable Good Life Catering business continued to thrive.

|||||||||||||||||||||||||||||||||||||||||||| ||||||||||||||||||||||||||||||||||||||||||||

Local, sustainable, and organic foods were now, if not commonplace, certainly more available than ever before. Foodies were willing to pay top dollar to discover what a gifted chef could do with bison, morels, and microgreens. People were starting to understand how low-quality, highly processed foods are detrimental—to the land, to the people producing them, and to those who eat them—and more people were identifying themselves as locavores. Added to these shifting general preferences were the increasing number of films and articles calling out how factory-produced

and factory-prepared food was destroying our health, in particular the health of our children. Public school lunch programs were reviewed by concerned educators, parents, and the students themselves, and many now look at how economic and physical health will be improved by relying on more whole and local foods and less on highly processed and internationally sourced foods.

The educational aspect of Jenny's story has become more central to her work as a chef in recent years. The indelible link between knowing where your food comes from and how you feel about feeding that food to your body is now gaining national focus and celebrity spotlights. Long before First Lady Michelle Obama's kitchen garden or reality-TV programs such as Jaime Oliver's *Food Revolution*, Jenny was calling for children to be more engaged in growing and cooking the food they ate. She refined her vision and developed a solid approach to bringing kids into the kitchen through her work with the University of Minnesota. Jenny is the resident chef–educator for the University of Minnesota Landscape Arboretum's Learning Center. Part of the vision and mission of the arboretum is to bring advances in botany and plant biology to the local and personal level—and the kitchen is personal. Much of Jenny's work involves teaching adult cooks how to prepare whole foods, and she delights her culinary students by helping them make connections with her favorite local chefs and sustainable and organic farmers and producers. Jenny has designed classes for children around these same concepts and connections. She is one of a few chefs to demonstrate that if children are made a part of growing, harvesting, selecting, and preparing their own food, they are more likely to enjoy and savor the dishes prepared. If a child has watched the kale grow from a seed or has pulled the golden beet from the ground and has chopped it, cooked it, and seasoned it, then it's not too far a stretch to understand why that child will relish eating it—or will at least try it instead of turning up his or her nose. The ease of preparing Jenny's recipes also encourages this transformation of the family kitchen. The success of her methods was borne out when she and Jayme Anderson, the program manager of St. Paul's Community Design Center of Minnesota, coached a team of three high school students to the finals of the national Cooking Up Change contest, a healthy school lunch recipe contest organized by the Healthy Schools Campaign and the National Farm to School Network.

As a recipient of a Bush Leadership fellowship, which is enabling her to pursue a master's degree in public health nutrition at the University of Minnesota, Jenny is equipping herself with even more tools and experience to enlarge the scope and reach of her approach to cooking good food. She has come far—from the excitement of early lessons learned in her own childhood kitchen to teaching a team of young teens, propelling them to cook competitively under a national spotlight—and is determined to spread that kind of excitement and appreciation for wholesome cooking throughout schools and communities.

After so many successful years of cooking, creating recipes, and teaching with whole and earth-friendly foods, it is now an ideal time to bring the highlights of Jenny Breen's journey together in a book. Even as she has become a leader in the local food movement through organizational work and teaching, she knows the real joy of food is in the home kitchen. Through this book, you too will be able to share her joy of using local, sustainable approaches to cooking—the Good Life way. Jenny celebrates the full flavors of locally grown ingredients and loves showing cooks of all ages and levels of experience how easy and simple it is to create wholesome dishes with whole foods. With this book as your guide, you will soon be at ease toasting nuts for a perfect Golden Pecan–Rice Salad, roasting peppers over an open flame for Autumn Pasta with Tarragon and Cider Sauce, or snipping your own fresh cilantro to flavor Roasted-Squash Gratin with Cilantro Pesto. You will be confident that you are bringing dishes to the table that are good for you and your family— and good for your world as well. That is, indeed, *Cooking Up the Good Life*. Join the celebration.

The Family Kitchen

THE KITCHEN IS CONSIDERED
THE HEART OF THE HOME FOR
GOOD REASONS.

But busy contemporary schedules have many of us spending less time together within that center. We don't expect you to suddenly start making each and every meal a study in family dynamics, but with a little creativity and some planning we know you can find ways to bring family members together to share in creating a dish that you will all eat together. If you have kids, the kitchen can become one of the best living classrooms they will ever enter, and everyone has the opportunity to have fun while learning about food chemistry (this is what happens when you add yeast), applied math (two tablespoons is the same as one-eighth of a cup), and even color theory (see how your eye is drawn to the orange of the yam in the greens). Our favorite part of what happens in the family kitchen, though, is the stories, whether folk tales such as that found in the Three Sisters Salad recipe, sharing something that happened during your day as you chop herbs for the sauce, or retelling a family legend about crazy Uncle Billy while spreading cream cheese frosting over layers of carrot cake. More than food chemistry occurs when two or more gather in the kitchen to cook: together they create something that tastes wonderful and is nourishing not only for the body but for the heart. There is magic.

To ensure comfort, ease, and a minimum number of arguments and scuffles in the kitchen (and let's be honest, they will happen), you will want to equip your kitchen with the tools needed to prepare all of the recipes. We consider these the essential elements:

- **Measuring cups and spoons**.
- **Paring knives**. Their small size makes them perfect for small hands. Do not let young children use serrated knives: these are very dangerous.
- **Blender**. Great for making fruit smoothies, blenders are not so great for pesto, many sauces, and soups.
- **Food processor**. This tool is best for pâtés, pestos, and some soups, though it can be messy. Kids love pushing the buttons on food processors.
- **Wand or immersion blender**. Wands are great for soups and very reasonably priced. Carefully supervise kids using wands because the temptation to lift the blender head out of the liquid is strong and results in a royally splattered, and potentially hot, mess.
- **Pots and pans with lids**. You'll want several capacities, including one quart, two quarts, four quarts, and five quarts. We love cast iron because it is reliable, gets better with age, leaches iron into your food, and is affordable. We also recommend reasonably priced stainless steel (sometimes you can find good deals on whole sets). Always choose pots and pans with good weight.
- **Basic utensils**: spatulas, wooden spoons, whisks, can opener (kids love opening cans), pizza cutter, peeler (we don't suggest peeling carrots, just clean them to keep the good vitamins and fiber), rolling pin.
- **Mixing bowls of several sizes**.
- **Colander**.
- **Cookie cutters**. Remember, they can be used to cut more than cookies and are fun for cutting sandwiches, toast, polenta, and pie crusts.
- **Silicone pan liners**. These are great for eliminating sticky, hard-to-clean baking and roasting messes. We even use them for fish. They are easy to clean and can go in the top rack of the dishwasher.

The family that cooks together is more likely to enjoy eating the meal together. Schedules don't always make it feasible to prepare and eat every meal as a family—in fact, that is likely impossible for most of us. But we believe it is crucial that this basic yet life-sustaining act be returned to the top of the priority list. It need not be complicated or fancy, but sitting down together to a meal made of real, wholesome food goes a long way in sustaining us physically and emotionally. Think about setting aside a few

"More than food chemistry occurs when two or more gather in the kitchen to cook: **TOGETHER THEY CREATE SOMETHING THAT TASTES WONDERFUL** *and is nourishing not only for the body but for the heart.* **THERE IS MAGIC."**

meals each week during which you prepare and eat a dish together, then add a few more meals when you eat together, even if it is leftovers or a sandwich. Not only do our kids look forward to family meals but it is the one guaranteed time of day when we look each other in the eye (yes, sometimes with frustration—but face-to-face nonetheless). Important research (much of it from our own University of Minnesota School of Public Health) shows significant physical, social, and mental health benefits related to shared family meals. The evidence strongly indicates that the more frequently children

and adolescents eat meals with their families, the higher their self-esteem and the better their grades, and the lower their incidences of depression and drug use. The quality of their diets is also greatly improved the more they eat family meals. All these benefits, not to mention the lifelong cooking skills, delicious food, and deep family connections, are compelling reasons to cook and eat together as much as possible.

You should know that most kids are capable of doing much more than you might expect in the kitchen. Notes related to the family kitchen are included at the beginning of most of these recipes. Review each recipe and look for simple tasks that can be assigned to the younger cook ⊨ in your family. There is almost always something to measure or pour, and this simple activity can fully engage a child in the process of preparing food. Don't demand perfection from less experienced cooks. Let go of high expectations and the need for order, focusing instead on the fun, and it will be easy to share the tasks of cutting, chopping, measuring, and mixing that are required for nearly every recipe.

Miso–Sesame Pâté ❦

MAKES 3 CUPS

1 ½ inches ginger root, peeled and coarsely chopped

1 pound firm or extra-firm tofu

¼ cup toasted sesame oil

⅓ cup miso paste

3/4 to 1 cup roasted, unsalted tahini (whether you get thinner tahini from a Middle Eastern grocery store or thicker tahini from a co-op, be sure to completely stir in all the oil on top before using it)

1 tablespoon tamari

This pâté is a lovely and unusual combination of the creamy textures and mild flavors of tahini and tofu with the bite of ginger and the intensity of toasted sesame oil. It is great on hearty whole grain bread or as a dip for vegetables. It has a warm and soothing flavor: part Asian, part health food, all yummy.

Miso is a fermented soybean paste that adds a subtle, salty bite. It contains beneficial bacteria that are great for digestion. It is usually found refrigerated by the tofu or tempeh, and, like wine, there are many varieties fermented from different grains and beans for a range of flavors and heaviness. I enjoy mellow brown rice miso or garbanzo miso, but suggest experimenting with different choices. Miso, if properly sealed, can last forever in your refrigerator.

Puree the ginger in the food processor. Add the tofu, toasted sesame oil, miso, tahini, and tamari and blend until creamy. You will probably need to stop and scrape the bowl a few times. Pulsing will help make sure all the smaller pieces get blended in.

Squash–Pecan Pâté

MAKES 4 CUPS

2 medium butternut squash

2½ cups pecans

4 cloves garlic

2 teaspoons salt

1 tablespoon cumin

1 teaspoon coriander

1 pound firm or extra-firm tofu

2 tablespoons olive oil

Pâté is a very unusual use for cooked squash, but it works smashingly! The squash and the pecans are both sweet, but they combine opposite textures to create a dynamic mouth sensation. This pâté is a perfect complement to a rich meal and hearty bread on a cool fall evening, makes a simple sandwich spread in the afternoon, and is great as a dip with chips.

Preheat the oven to 400 degrees. Cut the squash in half lengthwise, scoop out the seeds, and place the squash facedown in a shallow baking pan. Pour in about a half inch of water. Bake the squash until the skin stays indented when you press it, about 40 to 50 minutes. Remove the squash from the oven, let it cool, and then scoop the meat out of the squash. (Another way to bake squash is to prick the skin with a fork and bake the whole squash in a baking pan until it is soft to the touch, which will take about an hour. Let the squash cool, and then you can easily open it, remove the seeds, and scoop the meat from the skin.)

Puree the pecans, garlic, salt, cumin, and coriander in a food processor. Add 3 cups of the baked squash, the tofu, and the olive oil. Puree until well blended.

THE FAMILY KITCHEN

Kids can have fun removing the seeds from the squash. It's a process that suits their enjoyment of handling all things gooey. Also, once the squash is baked and cooled, they can help to scoop it out of the skin.

Polenta with Tomato Jam ⚘

MAKES ABOUT 2 DOZEN

POLENTA:

3 cups water

1 teaspoon salt

1¹/₂ cups polenta or coarse cornmeal

TOMATO JAM:

2 tablespoons olive oil

1 small onion, diced

3 cloves garlic, minced

1 inch fresh ginger root, peeled and minced

2 jalapeños, seeded and minced

1 (28-ounce) can crushed tomatoes

¹/₄ cup maple syrup or sugar

1 teaspoon salt

Chèvre (optional)

Fresh thyme or microgreens (optional)

In my family, polenta is as loved as chips or crackers. It can be firm or soft, cut into any shape, and topped with just about anything—and it's corn! I use corn grown and ground by Greg Reynolds of Riverbend Farm. It is unlike any other cornmeal I have had. He uses a combination of a few heirloom corn varieties. The cornmeal is grainy and corny, while also as fluffy as flour. The tomato jam is sweet, spicy, and tangy all at once, and provides a perfectly balanced finish to the delectable polenta.

Bring the salted water to a boil, then slowly add the polenta, whisking regularly to remove lumps. Simmer the mixture and continue stirring it for about 5 minutes. Remove the polenta from the heat, pour it into an oiled 9×13-inch pan, and spread it so it is about a half inch thick. Let the polenta cool. Then cut it into the desired shapes using a cookie cutter or the rim of a glass.

Heat the olive oil in a medium skillet over medium-high heat and sauté the onion, garlic, ginger, and jalapeños for about 3 minutes. Reduce the heat to medium and add the tomatoes, maple syrup, and salt and simmer on very low heat until quite thick, about 30 to 40 minutes. Let the jam cool for at least 2 hours or overnight in the refrigerator if possible.

When the jam is cool, spoon it onto the cut polenta. To dress up this dish, you can top each piece with a small dollop of chèvre and a sprig of thyme or a pinch of microgreens.

Stuffed Grape Leaves ❦

MAKES 30 ROLLS

1 cup brown rice

2 tablespoons olive oil

1 small onion, diced

3 cloves garlic, minced

1 small eggplant or jicama, peeled and cut into 1/4-inch dice

1/4 cup finely chopped fresh dill (see Growing Green Flavor, page 64) or 2 tablespoons dried dill

2 teaspoons salt

2 tablespoons lemon juice

30 preserved grape leaves (about half of a 16-ounce jar)

Olive oil for drizzling over rolls (about 2 tablespoons)

THE FAMILY KITCHEN

My daughters used to call these rice pickles. The stuffing and rolling can be a fun activity for kids. Just be prepared for the rolls to be assorted shapes and sizes.

These are a variation of the traditional Greek dolmas, using brown instead of white rice, and including eggplant or jicama for a seasonal twist and added texture. Grape leaves are typically preserved in glass containers; you can find them at most co-ops and certainly at any Middle Eastern market.

If you happen to have grape vines growing nearby, either wild or on an arbor, they will work too. Make certain they haven't been subjected to chemical spraying. Pick leaves about the size of your palm (any larger than that and they're too tough). Wash them well and trim off the stems. Stack the leaves gently in a steamer rack set in a saucepan over water, cover, and steam over low heat for 20 minutes. Let the leaves cool, and then they will be ready to stuff and roll.

Cook the brown rice in 2 cups of water and set it aside (see Cooking Grains, page 48). Preheat the oven to 375 degrees and grease a baking sheet.

Heat the olive oil in a medium skillet over medium heat and sauté the onion and garlic until tender, about 3 minutes. Add the eggplant or jicama and sauté it until soft, about another 5 to 8 minutes. Add the dill, salt, lemon juice, and cooked rice. Remove from the heat and mix well.

Lay out a grape leaf with the rough vein side facing up and spoon about a tablespoon of filling into the center. Start rolling from the stem end. When you reach the middle of the leaf, fold the sides in and continue rolling to the tip of the leaf. Place the roll seam side down in the pan. When the pan is filled, drizzle the stuffed grape leaves with olive oil and bake them for about 20 to 25 minutes.

Sun-Dried Tomato Pâté ❀

4 cups sun-dried tomatoes

2 cups almonds, toasted (see Toasting Nuts, page 27)

8 cloves garlic

2 tablespoons olive oil

3 tablespoons coarsely chopped fresh basil or 1 1/2 tablespoons dried

1 teaspoon salt

This pâté is still a favorite way to use sun-dried tomatoes. They are sweet, rich, and delicious. This recipe is a rich combination of some of my favorite ingredients: fruity tomato with powerful basil, rounded out by smoky almond flavor.

Soak the tomatoes in very hot water until they are very moist and juicy, at least 20 minutes.

In a food processor, combine the almonds and garlic and grind well. Then add half of the tomatoes with some of the soaking liquid and pulse to break down most of the larger chunks. Add the olive oil, basil, salt, and remaining tomatoes and process into a paste. This pâté will be blended, but not necessarily creamy. The longer you puree it, the more spreadable and less chunky it will be. Add more water if the mixture seems too thick.

Red Lentil Pâté ❀

MAKES 5 CUPS

1 ½ cups red lentils

¼ cup olive oil

⅓ cup lemon juice

4 cloves garlic

2 teaspoons salt

1 tablespoon cumin

¼ bunch parsley

1 cup walnuts

This low-key version of hummus will win people over. The tender and creamy red lentils produce a nicely textured pâté and hold their own as a perfect base for good strong seasonings like cumin and garlic. They also cook much more quickly than garbanzo beans.

Cook the lentils in 4 cups of water (see Cooking Beans and Legumes, page 7). Red lentils, unlike their green cousins, will cook to soft quite quickly. After draining the lentils, combine them with the rest of the ingredients in a food processor and puree.

THE FAMILY KITCHEN

Anytime there are things to throw into the food processor, bring in the kids. It is a simple way for them to be involved. They'll enjoy watching ingredients transform and take ownership in what they're preparing.

Cooking Beans and Legumes

Beans and legumes are wonderful foods. They contain no cholesterol and are high in folate, potassium, iron, and magnesium. They also offer beneficial fats and soluble and insoluble fiber. Along with being inexpensive and really filling, beans and legumes are incredibly versatile and, best of all, great tasting.

As a rule of thumb, 1 cup of dried beans cooked in 3 cups of water will yield about 2½ to 3 cups of cooked beans. One pound of dried beans yields about 5 or 6 cups of cooked beans. A 15-ounce can of beans, drained, equals about 1½ cups of cooked beans. Cooking times can vary significantly, depending upon the bean or legume. For example, red lentils cook quite quickly, about thirty minutes until soft, whereas garbanzo beans can take up to four hours before they are tender.

Begin by rinsing the beans and discarding any that are discolored or badly formed. Check for debris such as small rocks or twigs and discard them. Then the beans need to soak; soaking dissolves the indigestible sugars that cause gas during digestion. Beans cook more quickly when they have been soaked covered in water overnight or for at least eight hours. You'll drain off the water in which the beans have soaked before cooking.

If you don't have time for a long presoak,

pinto beans

you can put your washed and cleaned beans in a small stockpot. Cover the beans with water by 3 inches and bring them to a boil over medium heat. Boil the beans for 10 minutes, cover them, and remove them from the heat. Let them soak for an hour. Drain the beans, and then proceed.

Combine the soaked beans and water in a 2-quart saucepan and bring to a boil over medium heat. Reduce the heat to low; cover the pan, leaving the lid slightly askew to vent steam; and simmer the beans for 40 to 45 minutes. Check the beans for doneness: Beans are done when they can be easily mashed between two fingers or with a fork. Remember that some beans will take longer to cook than others.

peas

Add salt or acidic ingredients, such as vinegar and tomatoes (and their juice), during the last few minutes of cooking, when the beans are just tender. I have found that if these ingredients are added too early, they slow the cooking process and toughen the beans.

To freeze cooked beans for later use, immerse them in cold water until cool, then drain well and freeze. You can do this in small portions and then thaw them as needed for recipes and meals.

Fiesta Roulades ⓥ

MAKES ABOUT 40 PIECES

2 cups dried black beans

1 small onion, chopped

1 cup diced tomatoes with their liquid (about half a 14-ounce can)

1 cup (about 1 bunch) chopped fresh cilantro (see Growing Green Flavor, page 64)

1 tablespoon chili powder

1 tablespoon cumin

1 tablespoon garlic powder

1 teaspoon salt

1 cup brown rice cooked in 2 cups water (see Cooking Grains, page 48)

1 cup salsa

6 (8- or 10-inch) whole wheat (or other whole grain) tortillas

1 cup sour cream (omit for vegan version)

Roulades are a favorite finger food to serve as an appetizer or as a part of a larger meal. The classic bean, rice, salsa, and sour cream combination makes it a winner every time, for kids and adults alike. It combines the visual spiral of colors with a great balance of flavors for a savory bite (or two).

Cook the beans in 5 cups of water. Check midway through cooking to make certain there is plenty of water. You may need to add more water near the end of cooking. The beans should be soft, but not mushy. (See Cooking Beans and Legumes, page 7.) When the beans are almost cooked (approximately 50 minutes), add the onions, tomatoes with their liquid, half the cilantro, and the chili powder, cumin, garlic powder, and salt. Let simmer until the beans are soft and the liquid is well absorbed. Remove from the heat and combine the beans with 2 cups of cooked rice and the salsa. The mixture should be moist but fairly firm, not runny.

To assemble the roulades, spread a tortilla with a thin layer of sour cream and then thinly spread some bean mixture over the sour cream to cover about 2/3 of the tortilla. Sprinkle some cilantro over the beans, or use microgreens or salad greens to fill it out. Carefully roll up the tortilla. The sour cream should work as a glue to hold the tortilla closed. With a sharp knife (serrated knives work well), slice the ends off and then cut the rest of the roll into half-inch slices.

THE FAMILY KITCHEN

Here is perfect opportunity for kids to have fun with rolling. If they are old enough, they can do the slicing too; otherwise, a grown-up can do it. You can set up an assembly line at the counter, letting them place the ingredients in a tortilla and roll them up. It is hard for anyone to make these look bad!

Roasted Figs with Gorgonzola

MAKES 12

12 figs

6 ounces gorgonzola cheese

Honey

Rosemary

Roasted figs are a simple and elegant appetizer, or a light dessert for a hearty meal. The vibrant cheese flavor is complemented by the sweet and meaty figs. Of course, fresh figs are ideal, but dried will work. If you use dried, try to find figs that still have some moistness to them by pressing to see if they are soft. If they are not, they are too dry to use in this recipe.

Preheat the oven to 350 degrees. Cut the stem off each fig and then cut an X into it. Stuff a portion of gorgonzola about the size of a fingertip into the slit. Bake for 10 minutes.

To serve, drizzle honey on each plate and rest a stuffed fig on the honey. Add a garnish of rosemary.

THE FAMILY KITCHEN

Little hands love stuffing things, and stuffing cheese into the tiny openings of the figs will be a fun way for kids to help.

Mushroom Pâté ❀

MAKES 4 CUPS

1 cup cashews

1 cup walnuts

6 cloves garlic

1 pound button mushrooms (about 24 medium sized), crumbled by hand

1 teaspoon salt

¼ cup olive oil, if needed

This is the pâté that made me realize that nuts and vegetables might just be the most heavenly combination ever. Mushrooms have an amazing texture for this kind of thing. They offer firmness, creaminess, and an earthy flavor. This flavor, combined with the cashews and walnuts, makes a rich and hearty pâté. If you do use olive oil, make certain it is extra-virgin because its fresh flavor will enhance the strong flavors of the mushrooms and nuts. This pâté, with its refreshing spring flavor, is a great spread for crackers, bread, or chips.

Puree the cashews, walnuts, and garlic in a food processor until finely ground. Then add the mushrooms and salt and pulse for several minutes to blend all of the ingredients. You will need to keep scraping the bowl of the food processor to make certain that most of the pieces of the mushrooms get pureed. This pulsing and scraping can take several minutes. If the pâté seems too dry for your taste, add the olive oil and continue to pulse.

Artichoke Pâté ✳

MAKES 3 CUPS

2 (14-ounce) cans (5 cups) artichoke hearts, drained

¹/4 cup lemon juice

6 cloves garlic

Artichoke hearts are surprisingly rich tasting while being healthfully fat free. This simple and elegant pâté gains its sprightly and light flavor from the lemon and its bite and depth from the garlic. It is incredibly simple.

Combine the artichoke hearts, lemon juice, and garlic in a food processor and blend. Even though there is no fat in this pâté, it will have a creamed consistency.

Sunflower Seed Pâté

MAKES 4 TO 5 CUPS

4 cups unsalted sunflower seeds

1/2 cup olive oil

1 small red onion

2 tablespoons coarsely chopped fresh basil (see Growing Green Flavor, page 64) or 1 tablespoon dried

1/3 cup cider vinegar

1 teaspoon salt

1 pound firm tofu

1/3 cup water

Sunflower seeds seem to get overlooked other than as additions to salads and granola, and yet they offer a complex and unique flavor. They are kind of nutty but have an almost vegetable quality, and are a great source of calcium to boot. They are also generally kid friendly. I love this spread for crackers

Combine all the ingredients except the water in a food processor and puree 2 to 3 minutes. With the machine running, add the water slowly as needed to achieve a smooth consistency. The longer you puree, the smoother the pâté gets.

THE FAMILY KITCHEN

You can be certain most kids will enjoy making any pâté because it involves using a food processor to magically convert ingredients as familiar as sunflower seeds into something entirely different.

Stuffed Mushrooms ✿

30 fresh mushrooms, washed and dried

2 cups fresh basil leaves (see Growing Green Flavor, page 64)

3 cloves garlic

1/2 cup walnuts

2 tablespoons olive oil

1 teaspoon salt

8 ounces extra-firm tofu

Mushrooms have a nice spring flavor that is rich yet subtle. Choose extra-large mushrooms since they will shrink when baked. And you want to be able to fit a good amount of stuffing inside. The stuffing is rich and full of pungent flavors. Tofu is a great base for the stuffing because it is a blank canvas, taking whatever flavor we have to offer.

Preheat the oven to 375 degrees. Stem the mushrooms and set the caps aside.

Combine the basil, garlic, walnuts, olive oil, salt, and 1 cup of mushroom stems in a food processor and puree until fairly creamy. Add the tofu and puree until incorporated. The mixture can be left slightly chunky and textured.

Place the mushroom caps upside down on a baking pan and, using a small spoon, fill each one so the filling mounds up just over the edge. You can smooth the filling or leave it rough, as you prefer. Bake until the mushrooms are wrinkled and the filling is browned, about 20 minutes. Baking will create some moisture in the pan, so it is a good idea to remove the mushrooms from the pan immediately after taking them out of the oven.

THE FAMILY KITCHEN

Kids' little hands are perfect for placing just the right amount of stuffing into each mushroom. Who knows, after stuffing the little round caps, they may even be willing to try eating one.

Chicken Satay with Peanut Sauce

MAKES 18 PIECES

SATAY:

2 pounds of boneless chicken breasts

18 (6-inch) bamboo skewers

PEANUT SAUCE:

1 cup peanut butter (chunky or smooth, as you prefer)

1½ cups coconut milk

1 inch fresh ginger, peeled and minced

1 teaspoon turmeric

1 teaspoon chili powder

1 tablespoon cumin

2 teaspoons ground coriander

1 teaspoon cinnamon

1 cup apple juice

1 teaspoon salt

This is a simple way to prepare chicken or other meat in a flavorful way. The coconut milk is rich and creamy, without adding too much heaviness. Serve the satay alongside a stir fry or a salad for a perfect meal, or take it to a picnic along with other fun finger foods.

Cut the chicken breasts into long, thin pieces about 1 inch wide and 2 to 2½ inches long. Insert a bamboo skewer lengthwise into each strip of chicken. Place the skewered chicken in a deep baking pan. The chicken pieces can overlap, but try not to overlap more than one layer.

Whisk together the peanut butter, coconut milk, ginger, turmeric, chili powder, cumin, coriander, cinnamon, apple juice, and salt. Pour the sauce over the skewered chicken (avoid covering the wood ends of the skewers with sauce) and marinate for at least two hours, turning the skewers once or twice to coat all sides. The chicken can marinate overnight. Just cover it with plastic and place it in the refrigerator.

Preheat the oven to 375 degrees. Bake the chicken for about 15 minutes (you can bake it in the same pan it marinated in), then turn the chicken over, leaving a little space between the pieces so they don't stick together. Return the pan to the oven and bake for another 15 minutes. You can also cook the satay on the grill.

THE FAMILY KITCHEN

My kids call satay chicken on a stick. Kids will have fun putting the meat on the skewers and pouring the marinade over top. Be sure to remind them about the sharp skewer points and help devise a safe technique for skewering.

Tofu "Egg" Salad

MAKES 4 CUPS

2 pounds firm tofu

1½ cups soy mayonnaise

1½ tablespoons mustard (I prefer stone ground, but yellow and Dijon work nicely too)

2 tablespoons celery seed

1 tablespoon dill

2 teaspoons salt

2 teaspoons turmeric

3 stalks celery, diced small

½ cup small whole capers, rinsed and drained

¼ red onion, minced

It is actually hard to tell the difference between this and real egg salad. The texture is perfect and the color works; it satisfies vegans, kids, and everyone else. Although this recipe calls for celery, capers, and onion, you can add any stray vegetables you want to use up. So shred that lonely carrot and shell the last peas off your vines and toss them in. This salad is a simple and fun way to use things up and is great for a picnic when you need a little flexibility.

Mash the tofu in a bowl with a fork. In a separate bowl, combine the mayonnaise, mustard, celery seed, dill, salt, and turmeric. Mix well and add to the tofu. Add the celery, capers, and onion and stir to combine.

THE FAMILY KITCHEN

Give the kids a fork and let them go at the tofu, mashing to their delight.

Carrot–Cashew Pâté 🌱

MAKES 5 CUPS

3 cups carrots, chopped

1 cup unsalted cashews

2 cloves garlic

1/2 tablespoon miso paste

1 teaspoon celery seed

1/2 teaspoon salt

This may be the most popular pâté I have ever invented. It is colorful, creamy, sweet, and addicting. It is rich, but light enough to keep eating. An ideal summer spread, carrot–cashew pâté goes great with almost anything and brightens up any meal. The miso adds a subtle, yet flavorful touch (for more about miso, see Miso–Sesame Pâté, page 1).

Cook the carrots in a steamer set over water until they are very soft. Drain (reserving 1/2 cup of the cooking water) and set aside.

In a food processor, chop the cashews and garlic. Add the miso paste, carrots, celery seed, and salt. Add the reserved water a little at a time. Puree until well blended and creamy. You may need to pulse this mixture in the processor and scrape several times to capture all the small carrots pieces that get missed. Or, just leave them—they can be a fun, sweet surprise.

THE FAMILY KITCHEN

This is definitely a recipe to please children. Kids love carrots, but they are not used to seeing them as a spread, so the transformation is exciting. They can spread this pâté on crackers, toast, bagels, vegetable sticks, chips, or fresh baguette slices.

Dilled Veggie Pâté ❦

MAKES 4 CUPS

¼ red onion, coarsely chopped

2 cloves garlic

1 stalk celery, coarsely chopped

2 pounds medium or firm tofu

¼ cup olive oil

2 tablespoons cider vinegar

¼ cup fresh dill (see Growing Green Flavor, page 64) or 2 tablespoons dried

½ tablespoon stone-ground mustard

¼ teaspoon pepper

1 teaspoon salt

Here's a great alternative to ordinary sour cream–based dressings. It's also a great way to get your protein—without the fat or dairy—and still enjoy the crisp and fresh taste of dill. Most people either don't notice or don't mind that this is a tofu-based dip.

Chop the onion, garlic, and celery in a food processor. When well chopped, add the tofu, olive oil, vinegar, dill, mustard, pepper, and salt and blend well.

Smoked Trout and Potato Croquettes

MAKES ABOUT 3 DOZEN

2 pounds (about 8) red or yellow potatoes, chopped

4 ounces butter or olive oil (optional)

1 onion, chopped

1 tablespoon olive oil for sautéing

6 to 8 eggs

12 ounces smoked trout, skinned and boned

2 tablespoons minced fresh rosemary (see Growing Green Flavor, page 64) or 1 tablespoon dried

Salt and pepper

1 to 2 cups cornmeal

2 tablespoons vegetable oil (peanut oil works well because it has a high smoke point) for frying (optional)

I started buying smoked and fresh trout when my business partner, Karn Anderson, and I opened the Good Life Café in 1996. It is fun to find interesting and delicious ways to highlight the tender, smoky flavor of the trout, which is easily available from sustainable sources. I have been using Star Prairie smoked trout for more than fifteen years. It is a family-owned sustainable fish farm on the Apple River in Star Prairie, Wisconsin. The fish are caught and smoked weekly, so my order is placed before the fish are caught. They are always tender, fresh, and delicious. It is rewarding and satisfying to know that you are both supporting a small, family-run business whose values you share and using a fresh, high-quality product. You can taste the difference. These croquettes can be fancy as appetizers, casual as burgers, or anything in between. They are delicious alone, with greens or grains, or on a fresh bun with condiments.

Cook the potatoes in boiling water until soft and drain off the water. Mash as for mashed potatoes, adding the butter or olive oil if desired. Set aside.

Sauté the onions in a tablespoon of olive oil until they are translucent. Combine the onions, eggs, trout, and rosemary with the potatoes and mix well. Add cornmeal as needed to thicken the consistency. You should be able to form a solid but moist ball with your hands. Add salt and pepper to taste. Form into golf ball–sized balls or slightly larger patties. Fry the croquettes in hot oil until they are evenly browned or bake them in a 375 degree oven until brown (about 20 to 25 minutes).

Serve with goat cheese or aioli (you can mix fresh garlic or herbs into your favorite mayonnaise to make a perfect aioli for these or any other burgers).

THE FAMILY KITCHEN

Get the kids to help mash the potatoes, crumble the fish, and roll the mixture into balls or flatten it into patties.

Grilled Polenta with Three-Pepper Salsa ⓥ

⁙⁙⁙

MAKES 20 TO 24 PIECES, DEPENDING ON THE SIZE OF THE POLENTA PIECES

POLENTA:

2 cups polenta

5 cups water

2 teaspoons salt

1 cup grated Parmesan or Asiago or crumbled feta (omit for vegan version)

SALSA:

6 bell peppers of assorted colors (green, red, yellow), diced small

2 to 3 hot peppers, minced

1 red onion, minced

4 cloves garlic, minced

4 tomatoes, minced

1/2 cup (about 1/2 bunch) minced fresh cilantro

1/4 cup lemon or lime juice

2 teaspoons salt

FOR SERVING:

1 pound queso fresco or other soft cheese, crumbled (omit for vegan version)

Polenta is a versatile treat and works in a variety of settings. I use it in everything from salads to pizzas to appetizers. The salsa is a colorful, zesty, and crisp contrast to the soft and creamy polenta. This dish will shake up your concept of a grilled meal.

In a saucepan, heat the water until boiling. Slowly pour in the polenta while stirring. Lower the heat and continue to stir. Add the salt and cheese, if desired, and continue to stir. After about 10 minutes, remove the polenta from the heat and pour it into an oiled 9 × 13-inch baking dish or two pie pans (any pan will work). Spread it evenly about 1 inch thick and let it cool while preparing the salsa.

Combine all of the salsa ingredients in a large bowl and mix well. If you want a smoother consistency, remove half the mixture and puree it in a food processor or a blender. Mix the puree into the remaining salsa mixture.

Cut the cooled polenta into any shape you desire. Triangles or circles are nice. Brush both sides with olive oil and place on a hot grill. Grill until grill marks show (about 5 minutes), flip, and grill the other side. Place crumbled cheese (if using) on the polenta for the last minute so it will melt. Serve topped with salsa.

Balsamic Vinaigrette ⓥ

MAKES ABOUT 2 CUPS

²/₃ cup olive oil

3/4 cup balsamic vinegar

3/4 cup raspberry wine vinegar

1 tablespoon Dijon mustard

2 tablespoons honey (use apple juice or maple syrup for vegan version)

1 tablespoon minced fresh thyme or 1¹/₂ teaspoons dried

1 tablespoon finely chopped fresh basil

1 tablespoon finely chopped fresh oregano or 1¹/₂ teaspoons dried

1 teaspoon salt

This classic combination requires good extra-virgin olive oil and high-quality balsamic vinegar, such as one from Modena. Add a little honey to balance the tartness and some raspberry vinegar for a nice fruity infusion. The fresh herb flavor is central to the taste, and if you grow herbs indoors, you will always have a supply handy (see Growing Green Flavor, page 64).

Place all the ingredients in a bowl and whisk well. Keep the vinaigrette in the refrigerator. In addition to dressing greens, this vinaigrette is wonderful as a dip for crusty bread.

THE FAMILY KITCHEN

Measuring and pouring is always fun for kids. This recipe offers an opportunity to discuss ingredients at a deeper level: you can talk about the independence that cooking your own food offers, and, in the case of salad dressing, you can talk about how you are no longer dependent upon expensive bottled choices that include loads of additional ingredients that are not generally nutritious or pure.

Roasted Garlic-Tomato Sauce ✳

MAKES 6 TO 8 CUPS

16 cloves garlic, 8 whole and 8 minced

3 tablespoons olive oil

2 medium onions, sliced thin

1/2 cup champagne vinegar

8 cups diced fresh tomatoes with their liquid (if necessary, substitute a 14-ounce can per 2 cups diced tomatoes)

1/4 cup maple syrup

1/4 cup minced fresh thyme (see Growing Green Flavor, page 64) or 1 tablespoon dried

1/4 cup minced fresh oregano or 1 tablespoon dried

2 teaspoons salt

This very fresh tomato sauce is a lovely and simple way to use all those beautiful tomatoes that are ripening on your countertop or arrived in your CSA delivery. The roasted garlic adds lots of body and flavor. The tomatoes, with their natural sweetness and the addition of maple syrup, blend into autumn nectar. Use tomatoes in a variety of colors (yellow, green, orange) for a visually striking sauce. Serve with pasta or chicken or tofu—or just eat it by itself, it's that delicious.

Preheat the oven to 400 degrees. Peel the 8 whole garlic cloves and brush them with 1 tablespoon of the olive oil. Place them on a shallow baking sheet and roast them for 12 to 15 minutes, until they are brown on the outside and very soft. Set them aside.

In a large pot, sauté the onions and the minced garlic in 2 tablespoons of olive oil over medium heat. After three minutes, add the vinegar, tomatoes, maple syrup, thyme, oregano, and salt. Simmer for 15 to 20 minutes. Remove 1 cup of sauce from the pot and puree it with the roasted garlic. Return the pureed sauce to the pot and simmer for another 20 minutes.

Basil—Walnut Pesto and Cilantro—Pecan Pesto

MAKES 2 CUPS

BASIL—WALNUT PESTO:

3 cups fresh basil leaves
(see Growing Green Flavor,
page 64)

2/3 cup walnuts (pecans,
almonds, hazelnuts,
sunflower seeds, or
traditional pine nuts may
be used in place of walnuts
for variety)

6 cloves garlic

1/4 cup olive oil

1 teaspoon salt

CILANTRO—PECAN PESTO:

3 cups (about 3 bunches)
cilantro leaves (see Growing
Green Flavor, page 64)

2 cups pecans (or almonds)

6 cloves garlic

1/3 cup olive oil

1 teaspoon salt

Basil—walnut pesto is a classic, never to go out of style. I adapt it slightly by omitting the Parmesan and find that it is never missed. The basil is so aromatic and rich, the garlic has a nice bite, and the walnuts are oily and just bitter enough to make a perfect paste. In the cilantro—pecan pesto, the cilantro is actually subtle, the garlic does its thing, and the pecans add just enough sweetness to balance the bite of the garlic.

Pesto is open to interpretation. If you have fresh herbs, fresh garlic, good olive oil, and nuts, you can hardly go wrong. Anything else is simply embellishment and adds to the uniqueness of the taste. I always encourage students to experiment with different nuts or herbs or new things altogether, like sun-dried tomatoes or olives. The sky really is the limit.

Basil—walnut pesto: Combine all of the ingredients in a food processor. Blend until well mixed. Store this pesto in the refrigerator or freeze portions for later use.

Cilantro—pecan pesto: Combine all of the ingredients in a food processor and blend until smooth. Refrigerate until needed.

THE FAMILY KITCHEN

Kids can help by picking all the basil or cilantro leaves off the stems. Then they can help put everything into the food processor and watch it transform into one of the most kid-friendly sauces ever.

Lemony Olive Sauce with Grilled Vegetables ⚘

MAKES 8 TO 12 SERVINGS

1/2 cup olive oil

2 tablespoons honey (use agave syrup for vegan version)

Juice of 2 lemons

Zested rind of one lemon

4 cloves garlic, finely chopped

1 teaspoon minced fresh fennel greens

6 cups seasonal vegetables such as beets, onions, green beans, and zucchini, peeled (if desired) and sliced in large, thin pieces

Citrus is always a wonderful way to bring out the flavors of vegetables. These autumn flavors are enhanced by the tanginess of the lemon and the savoriness of the olives. The honey ties these two flavors together nicely; so, like autumn, there is a combination of sweet and sour, plus the wonderful rich sensation of umami—a Japanese word for a fifth flavor that goes beyond sweet, sour, salty, or bitter. In addition, this is a lovely looking sauce that complements rich green and orange vegetables.

Whisk together the olive oil, honey, and lemon juice. Stir in the lemon zest, garlic, and fennel. Place the cut veggies in the sauce and marinate for up to 4 hours.

Remove the vegetables from the marinade and reserve the leftover marinade. Place the veggies on a hot, oiled grill and turn as needed. Using a grill basket or grill wok will make grilling easier. Top with the remaining sauce before serving.

Lemon–Miso Sauce ❦

MAKES ABOUT 5 CUPS

2 (14-ounce) cans coconut milk

1/2 cup miso paste

1 cup lemon juice (about 6 medium lemons)

1/2 cup apple juice

With its unusual combinations of flavors, this simple sauce is surprisingly extraordinary. The lemon juice and miso offer great tartness, yet very different flavors: the deep fermented flavor of miso is the opposite of the lively and light lemon (for more about miso, see Miso–Sesame Pâté, page 1). Adding coconut milk turns things sideways. The coconut milk is rich and sweet and also provides fat to thicken and bind the sauce. The simplicity is the most beautiful thing of all. This is an excellent sauce for stir-fries, fish, chicken, or greens.

Blend all of the ingredients in a food processor, or whisk by hand until smooth. Store the sauce in the refrigerator.

Sweet Almond Curry Sauce ❦

MAKES 6 CUPS

3 cups roasted almonds
(see Toasting Nuts)

8 cloves garlic

1 tablespoon turmeric

2 teaspoons cumin

2 teaspoons coriander

2 teaspoons chili powder

1¹/₂ teaspoons salt

2 cups apple juice

2 cups orange juice
(about 6 medium oranges)

1 cup water

This sauce fully highlights the texture and flavor of almonds. They bring a sweetness and flavor loved by almost everyone. The orange juice adds sweetness, so the curry's spiciness is more gentle and savory than hot. This is a great sauce for vegetables, stir-fries, and even pasta. You can control the texture of this sauce—from smooth to crunchy, depending on your preference—by how long you let the food processor run.

Puree the almonds and garlic in a food processor until fine. Add the turmeric, cumin, coriander, chili powder, and salt and blend. Add the apple juice, orange juice, and water slowly until well blended. This sauce will keep in the refrigerator for a few weeks. You can also freeze small portions for later use.

THE FAMILY KITCHEN

This recipe is kid friendly. Not only is it fun to make, but it introduces some of the flavors of curry and spices without burning their young mouths.

Toasting Nuts

Toasting brings out a deeper, richer flavor in nuts. There are two ways to toast nuts—in a skillet or in the oven. First, make certain the nuts are shelled and of uniform size.

You can toast nuts in a heavy skillet over medium heat until they start to become golden. Turn them constantly so they don't scorch. This usually takes five to seven minutes. Toast only as many nuts as will cover the bottom of the skillet at one time. You'll begin to notice an almost sweet caramel fragrance from the nuts when they're ready. If you are careful and attentive, you can get the nuts very well toasted and bring out their wonderful aroma with a slow, medium heat. Be careful not to let them sit without moving or they will burn.

You can also toast nuts in the oven. Spread the nuts in an even layer in a shallow baking pan. Roast the nuts at 400 degrees for about ten minutes, stirring and turning after five minutes.

Since nuts contain their own oil, there is no need to add any when toasting. This is also true when preparing nut butters. The natural oils that are released during toasting help to break down the nuts into delicious, creamy nut butter. To make nut butter, simply grind toasted nuts in a food processor (a coffee or spice grinder will work for smaller quantities) until they become creamy, usually about three to five minutes. You may need to stop and scrape the bowl once or twice. Add salt if desired. Two cups of nuts will yield about one cup of nut butter. You can combine different nuts for fantastic flavors. My favorites are almond–pecan and cashew–walnut.

To have a ready supply of toasted nuts at hand, toast a large quantity at the same time and store what you don't use in an airtight jar. You can store them on the shelf for up to two months or in the freezer (I use heavy-duty freezer bags) for up to six months.

almonds

walnuts

Savory Peanut Sauce

MAKES 3 CUPS

1 cup smooth peanut butter

1½ cups coconut milk

1 cup apple juice

1 teaspoon turmeric

1 teaspoon chili powder

1 tablespoon cumin

2 teaspoons coriander

1 teaspoon cinnamon

1 teaspoon salt

Winter sauces are heavy and rich. These are great qualities for warming cold bodies and spirits. This sauce uses coconut milk and peanuts, which is a traditional combination. What is unique about this sauce is the cinnamon. It brings a new edge to the savory character of this sauce.

Combine all of the ingredients in a bowl and whisk until creamy.

THE FAMILY KITCHEN

Kids love this sauce! It is fun for them to use peanut butter in a sauce. If there is a peanut allergy, soy butter, sunflower butter, and tahini are fine substitutes. It is great with noodles and rice, and may even inspire more vegetable eating when served as a dipping sauce.

Roasted Red Pepper and Leek Sauce ⓥ

MAKES ABOUT 3 CUPS

6 red bell peppers

¹/₄ cup olive oil, plus additional for roasting peppers

2 large leeks, chopped

5 cloves garlic

2 teaspoons salt

¹/₄ cup sherry vinegar

2 to 2¹/₂ cups milk, cream, or buttermilk (use soy milk for vegan version)

This is a somewhat unusual use for leeks and sherry vinegar. The peppers add a roasted and sweet flavor, the sautéed leeks are also sweet and creamy, and the vinegar has a mild bite. The sauce is colorful and perfect for croquettes, vegetables, or even fish.

Preheat the oven to 400 degrees. Brush the red peppers with olive oil and roast them in the oven until the skin is black and charred, about 5 to 7 minutes. The peppers can also be roasted over an open flame, such as a gas burner. Using tongs, carefully hold the pepper about an inch away from the flame and gently rotate it until it is charred all over, about 2 minutes per side. Whichever method you use, immediately place the roasted peppers in a closed paper bag for about 10 minutes to cool. When cool, remove the peppers' skins, stems, and seeds.

Sauté the leeks and garlic in ¹/₄ cup of olive oil until the leeks are soft and wilted. Scrape the leek mixture into a food processor and add the peppers and salt. Puree while slowly adding the vinegar and milk until the sauce is the desired consistency and well blended.

Cashew–Orange Sauce ❦

MAKES ABOUT 5 CUPS

3 cups cashews

3 cups fresh orange juice
(about 9 medium oranges)

2 tablespoons tamari

4 cloves garlic

1 tablespoon cumin

2 teaspoons chili powder

2 teaspoons cinnamon

2 teaspoons celery seed

Cashews have a unique property in that when pureed, they attain a milky and creamy consistency. They are sweet and nutty too. Combine this with sweet orange juice and celery seed for a slightly offbeat, savory flavor. This sauce is excellent over roasted poultry or broiled fish and also works well with pasta or stir-fried vegetables.

Puree the cashews in a food processor until well processed and almost turned into cashew butter. (Incidentally, this is how cashew butter is made. You need not add anything to it, just puree the cashews, stopping occasionally to scrape the bowl, and eventually you will get a delicious savory nut butter.) Add the remaining ingredients and process.

Garlic–Pecan Sauce *

MAKES ABOUT 5 CUPS

3 cups toasted pecans (see Toasting Nuts, page 27)

2 teaspoons salt

8 cloves garlic

2 cups orange juice (about 6 medium oranges)

1¹/₂ cups apple juice

1 teaspoon cinnamon

1 to 2 cups water, as needed (or substitute milk for a creamier texture)

This recipe combines the creamy sweetness of toasted pecans with the bite of fresh garlic for a wonderful nut-based sauce that is great for stir-fries, steamed vegetables, pasta, and even fish.

Puree all of the ingredients except the water in a food processor. With the machine running, add only as much water as needed to reach the desired consistency.

Ginger–Sesame Sauce *

MAKES ABOUT 2 CUPS

¹/₄ cup minced garlic (about 10–12 medium cloves)

¹/₄ cup minced fresh ginger root (about 2 inches, peeled)

¹/₄ cup plus 2 tablespoons toasted sesame oil

¹/₄ cup tamari

¹/₃ cup lemon juice (about 1 medium lemon)

¹/₄ cup maple syrup

In this sauce, the earthy flavors of toasted sesame oil and tamari and the bite of ginger and lemon are balanced by maple syrup. It is simple, nutritious, and creamy but unusual enough that it isn't just the same old sauce. It's likely you'll have all the ingredients at hand, and it is quick to prepare. It is delicious on vegetables, grains, and noodles or as a marinade for chicken and fish.

Sauté the ginger and garlic in 2 tablespoons of sesame oil for 2 to 3 minutes to infuse the oil with their flavor. Set aside. Whisk the ¹/₄ cup of sesame oil with the tamari, lemon juice, and maple syrup. Then add the cooled ginger and garlic. This sauce keeps very well in the refrigerator for a long time.

THE FAMILY KITCHEN

Kids ages 6 and older can do most of this recipe without any help. It is a great way to practice using measuring cups.

Salsa Fresca ❦

MAKES 6 CUPS

4 large tomatoes, finely diced

1 small red or white onion, finely diced

8 cloves garlic, finely diced

1 small red or yellow bell pepper, finely diced

1/2 cup (about 1/2 bunch) finely chopped cilantro (see Growing Green Flavor, page 64)

1/4 cup lemon juice (about 1 medium lemon)

1 to 11/2 teaspoons salt

A warm summer day is made complete with a bowl of fresh salsa. Bell pepper, fresh cilantro, and lots of garlic make this well-known classic more colorful. There are endless variations to this kind of salsa, and even the type of tomato you use will affect the flavor—choose different types and colors of tomatoes to make this salsa an even more flavorful celebration of summer.

Combine all the ingredients in a bowl and mix well. For seasonal variations, add 1 cup of fresh corn, 1 cup of cooked black beans, 1 cup of diced ripe avocado, or 1 cup of diced fresh fruit (such as pear, pineapple, or orange).

THE FAMILY KITCHEN

Choose different types of tomatoes from the garden, farmers' market, or another local source and see if you can taste the difference. Ask each other what makes each tomato different: Are some sweeter? Do some taste like other fruits, such as strawberries or melon? Do some taste like their color? Have everyone close their eyes and do a taste test. Of course, kids can also help with much of the chopping and mixing.

Barbecue Sauce for Tempeh, Mock Duck, or Chicken ⓥ

MAKES 5 CUPS OF SAUCE;
BARBECUED PROTEIN
SERVES 6 TO 10

This barbecue sauce is rich and tangy with molasses and miso and enhanced with lots of lemon, cider vinegar, and garlic. Not only does it work perfectly as a grilling sauce, it also works well in the oven. It is dense enough to enhance tempeh, mock duck, chicken, or even pork.

SAUCE:

1¹/₂ **cups minced onion**

9 **cloves garlic, minced**

2 **tablespoons corn or canola oil**

¹/₂ **cup miso paste**

1 **cup lemon juice (about 3 medium lemons)**

1 **cup cider vinegar**

1 **cup rice syrup or 3/4 cup maple syrup (for vegan version) or 3/4 cup honey**

¹/₂ **cup tamari**

3/4 **cup molasses**

3 **tablespoons chili powder**

2 **tablespoons prepared mustard**

PROTEIN:

3 **pounds tempeh or mock duck (for vegan version) or chicken**

Olive oil

Sauté the onion and garlic in the oil. Combine the miso paste, lemon juice, and vinegar and add it to the onion and garlic mixture. Add the syrup, tamari, molasses, chili powder, and mustard and mix well. Simmer for 30 to 40 minutes. You will have more sauce than you need for 3 pounds of barbecue. Freeze the extra for future use.

Preheat the oven to 375 degrees. Brown the tempeh, chicken, or mock duck in a small amount of olive oil, turning occasionally to brown evenly on all sides, about 8 to 10 minutes. Place in a large baking dish, cover with sauce, and bake for 30 minutes.

For grilling, use as you would any sauce: brush onto the protein and continue to brush on more as it cooks, turning regularly.

Italian Potato Soup

SERVES 8 TO 12

2 tablespoons olive oil

1 medium onion, sliced

3 carrots, sliced or diced

6 cloves garlic, minced

1 tablespoon minced fresh thyme (see Growing Green Flavor, page 64) or 2 teaspoons dried

1 tablespoon minced fresh rosemary or 2 teaspoons dried

1 tablespoon minced fresh oregano or 2 teaspoons dried

1 tablespoon garlic powder

2 teaspoons salt

8 medium potatoes (Yellow Finn and Yukon Gold are very nice), diced

8 cups vegetable stock or water (see Making Stock)

1/2 bunch kale or other dark, leafy greens such as collards, mustard, chard, or spinach, stemmed and chopped (optional)

2 to 3 cups coarsely chopped seasonal vegetables such as broccoli, peppers, or green beans (optional)

In autumn, the air is cooler and the vegetables are heartier. And one of the heartiest vegetables is the comforting potato. This soup uses potatoes as a base and gains texture with the addition of other seasonal vegetables. Italian seasonings enhance the potato flavor, resulting in a thick soup that is a perfect meal in a bowl.

Heat the olive oil in a stockpot and sauté the onions, carrots, and garlic, then add the thyme, rosemary, oregano, garlic powder, and salt. Add the potatoes and the stock or water. Cover and let simmer until the potatoes are very soft. Add the kale and other veggies, if using. Cover and simmer on low heat about 1 hour, stirring occasionally to make certain the soup doesn't burn.

THE FAMILY KITCHEN

Kids love soup. Perhaps it's because most soups have such a warm and comforting texture. Soups also allow you to add some vegetables or beans to a meal in a way that somehow simplifies them, making them kid friendly. Kids can help chop, mix, and measure. Encourage them to keep checking and stirring as the mixture transforms from raw ingredients into a warm meal.

Making Stock

My recipes often call for stock. Canned vegetable or meat stock certainly works fine, but making your own stock is easier than you might think, infinitely better tasting, and just a sensible approach to using up every last bit of goodness from your locally grown food. With a little planning, you can have fabulous homemade stock ready to enhance the flavor of almost any savory recipe asking for stock or water.

Vegetable Stock

The key to making vegetable stock is remembering to save many of your cooking remnants. Just toss the clean vegetable trimmings, from stems to stalks to peelings, into plastic zipper bags or plastic containers and keep them in the freezer until there is enough for the stock pot. Once you've accumulated enough veggie scraps to fill a gallon-size freezer bag, you're ready to make a batch of stock. You want to save:

- onion ends and skins
- ends of carrots, celery, potatoes, sweet potatoes, and beets
- garlic and ginger skins
- mushroom stems

The only things you don't want to put into a stock are foods from the brassica, or crucifer, family. Crucifers—including cabbage, arugula, broccoli, bok choy, Brussels sprouts, cauliflower, collards, kale, kohlrabi, mustard greens, Swiss chard, radishes, rutabagas, turnips, turnip greens, and watercress—will make the stock bitter and gas-producing.

Place all the vegetables trimmings together in a large stockpot—at least 4 quarts—and fill it with water. Ideally, you will have about a 1 to 3 ratio of vegetables to water. Cover the stockpot, set it over medium heat, and bring the pot to a boil. Maintain a rolling boil for about 30 minutes, then reduce the heat slightly to a simmer. Continue simmering the stock, covered, for 2 to 3 hours.

The goal is to reduce the stock considerably as it deepens in color and aroma. You really can't overcook stock—the more it cooks, the thicker and richer it will get. But after a good number of hours, remove the pot from the heat and let the stock cool. When it is well cooled, pour the stock into another container through a fine-meshed sieve (such as a chinois) or a colander lined with cheesecloth to remove all the vegetable debris. You can then measure this wonderful, dark, thick stock into smaller plastic containers and freeze it until needed. It helps to store it in 1- or 2-cup portions for cooking purposes. It can also be handy to freeze some in ice cube trays so you can add a cube or two to the steamer when you're cooking vegetables or when you need just a smidge of flavor and liquid to thin a sauce or gravy.

Another Soup Stock

If you want to prepare a stock using whole vegetables rather than scraps, try this recipe. It never fails.

1 large leek, rinsed and cut up	4 stems parsley
5 carrots, chopped in half	1 sprig fresh thyme
1 head garlic (at least 8 cloves)	8 peppercorns
2 red bell peppers	2 bay leaves
1 pound tomatoes	1 cup red wine
2 large onions	4 quarts water
2 tablespoons olive oil	$1/2$ cup sun-dried tomatoes
1 stalk celery, cut into about 3-inch lengths	2 teaspoons salt

Preheat the oven to 350 degrees. Coat the leek, carrots, garlic, peppers, tomatoes, and onions in olive oil and place them in a roasting pan. Roast the vegetables until they are well browned, about $1^{1}/4$ hours.

Wrap the celery, parsley, thyme, peppercorns, and bay leaves in cheesecloth and tie it closed to create a bouquet garni. After transferring the roasted veggies to a large stockpot, pour the wine into the roasting pan and stir with a wooden spoon to deglaze the pan. Scrape the wine and all the pan scrapings into the stockpot. Add the water, bouquet garni, sun-dried tomatoes, and salt. Then follow the instructions given above for cooking, straining, and storing stock.

Potato-Leek Soup ⓥ

SERVES 6 TO 8

1/4 cup olive oil

2 leeks, rinsed and sliced

6 to 8 medium potatoes, cubed

1 tablespoon garlic powder

2 tablespoons minced fresh dill (see Growing Green Flavor, page 64) or 1 tablespoon dried

2 teaspoons salt

4 to 6 cups water

2 cups milk or soy milk (for vegan version)

For me, potatoes are a harbinger of fall. Fresh potatoes and leeks are simmered with dill and pureed until smooth and creamy. The flavors are clean and earthy. Even when not using dairy, this soup has a lovely creamy texture.

Heat the olive oil in a stockpot and sauté the leeks, potatoes, garlic powder, dill, and salt. Add the water and simmer until the potatoes are very soft, about 20 minutes. Remove the soup from the heat and puree it in small batches, adding some of the milk to each batch. Return the soup to the pot and stir to blend. Or, if you have an immersion blender, simply puree the soup in the pot while slowing adding the milk. The soup should be very creamy.

THE FAMILY KITCHEN

Kids will enjoy peeling the layers of leeks apart and rinsing out all the hidden dirt. If they are older, they can use a paring knife to cut them. Potatoes are also fun to cut, and in a recipe like this, cutting them to a consistent size is not important.

Harvest Medley ❋

SERVES 8 TO 12

¹/4 cup olive oil

1 medium onion, diced

4 stalks celery, diced

4 cloves garlic, minced

1 medium butternut or
kabocha squash, peeled and
cut into 1-inch cubes

1 large yam, peeled and cut
into 1-inch cubes

3 large carrots, sliced or diced

1 tablespoon minced fresh
thyme (see Growing Green
Flavor, page 64) or 2
teaspoons dried

1 teaspoon celery seed

1 teaspoon turmeric

8 to 10 cups vegetable stock
(see Making Stock, page 38)

2 teaspoons salt

¹/2 pound green beans,
trimmed and cut in half (you
can use frozen if fresh are not
available)

1 medium red, yellow, or
orange bell pepper, coarsely
diced

*One of the predominant colors of autumn is orange. This recipe
will reveal how many degrees of golden color you can blend in
a soup pot. The result is a fragrant and lush soup that provides
what its rich color promises. Serve this with Maple or Pumpkin
Corn Bread (see page 148–49) and a plate of sliced apples and
cheese for a simple fireside meal.*

Heat the olive oil in a medium stockpot and sauté the onion,
celery, garlic, squash, yam, carrots, thyme, celery seed, and
turmeric. Add 4 cups of stock and the salt and simmer until
the squash and yams are soft, about 10 minutes. Add the green
beans and peppers and 4 to 6 more cups of stock or water.
Cover and simmer on low heat until the vegetables are tender,
about 20 to 25 minutes.

Turkey Soup with Herbed Dumplings

SERVES 8 TO 12

SOUP:

2 tablespoons olive oil

1 large onion, chopped

4 cloves garlic, minced

2 carrots, chopped

2 parsnips, chopped

1/2 head celery, chopped

2 teaspoons salt

1/4 cup minced fresh herbs, such as thyme, rosemary, and basil (see Growing Green Flavor, page 64)

6 cups chicken, turkey, or veggie stock (see Making Stock, page 38)

1/2 bunch kale or collards, stemmed and chopped (about 2 cups)

2 cups roasted turkey, diced, or a turkey carcass

6 cups water

Asiago (optional)

DUMPLINGS:

2 cups flour (a mix of 1 cup whole wheat and 1 cup unbleached flour will work)

1 tablespoon baking powder

1/4 cup butter or olive oil

1/2 cup milk or stock

1/4 cup minced fresh herbs, such as basil, sage, oregano, or thyme (pick one or mix them)

It's fun to say the word dumplings, and it's even more fun to eat them. Think of them as the down comforter version of the noodle. Dumplings are satisfying, easy to make, and, in my version, they contain special touches.

Heat the olive oil in a stockpot and sauté the onion, garlic, carrots, parsnips, celery, salt, and herbs. After about 3 minutes, add the stock and bring it to a boil. After 2 minutes, turn the heat down to simmer, add the turkey bones (if using), and cover the pot. Allow to simmer for about 30 minutes.

While the soup simmers, make the dumpling dough. Combine the flour and baking powder, then cut in the butter. Stir in the milk or stock and the herbs and mix until fully incorporated. The mixture will be doughy. Set the dough aside until the soup is ready.

When the liquid has reduced, add the 6 cups of water. If you used turkey bones, remove them and be sure to return any meat to the pot. If you're using roasted turkey, add it now, along with the kale or collards. Drop the dumplings by the tablespoonful into the soup. Cover the pot and let the soup simmer. After 15 minutes, remove the lid and check the dumplings—they should be floating. Serve with grated Asiago, if desired.

THE FAMILY KITCHEN

Dumplings are a lot like matzoh balls, which in my family are a much anticipated favorite in Bubbe's (Grandma's) house. Kids have a lot of fun mixing the dough, dropping the balls into the bubbling soup, and waiting and watching for them to bob to the top when they are cooked.

Southern-Style Squash Chili ✿

SERVES 8 TO 12

2 cups dried black-eyed peas

¼ cup olive oil

1 large onion, diced

1 medium butternut squash or 2 yams, peeled and cut into 1-inch cubes

4 cloves garlic, minced

1 tablespoon cumin

1 tablespoon chili powder

¼ cup minced fresh thyme (see Growing Green Flavor, page 64) or 2 tablespoons dried

2 teaspoons salt

8 cups water or vegetable stock (see Making Stock, page 38)

4 large tomatoes, diced

2 cups fresh or frozen corn kernels

4 cups spinach (or other greens), stemmed and chopped

¼ cup minced fresh cilantro (see Growing Green Flavor, page 64) or 2 tablespoons ground coriander

¼ cup tomato paste

¼ cup maple syrup

1 pound chicken breast, diced (omit for vegan version)

This chili has the basic chili formula (tomato base and beans) plus some unusual ingredients (squash or yams and spinach) to amp up the color, the nutritional value, and the texture. A kiss of maple syrup cuts the acid and pulls the flavors together. The creaminess of the squash adds a new dimension to a familiar food, introducing a novel twist just when things are getting old. It still works with all the traditional sides (guacamole, chips, sour cream, and cheese) and is delicious accompanied by hearty whole grain bread or corn chips or served over brown rice. Pumpkin Corn Bread (page 149) is also a perfect companion to this recipe.

Cook the black-eyed peas in 5 cups of water (see Cooking Beans and Legumes, page 7) and set them aside.

Heat the olive oil in a stockpot over medium heat. Sauté the onion, squash, garlic, cumin, chili powder, thyme, and salt, and then add 4 cups of water or stock. Cover the pot and simmer until the squash is soft, about 15 minutes. If using chicken, brown it in a skillet and add it to the pot along with the black-eyed peas, tomatoes, corn, spinach, cilantro, tomato paste, maple syrup, and remaining 4 cups of water or stock and simmer another 15 to 20 minutes.

Hearty Black Bean Soup ⚹

SERVES 12 TO 16

4 cups dried black beans

2 tablespoons olive oil

1 medium onion, sliced

8 cloves garlic, minced

4 carrots, sliced

1 bell pepper, diced

3 tomatoes, diced, or 1 (14-ounce) can diced tomatoes

1 tablespoon cumin

1 teaspoon salt

1 tablespoon chili powder

4 to 8 cups water or vegetable stock (see Making Stock, page 38)

1 cup tomato puree (or 1/2 cup tomato paste mixed with 1/2 cup water)

Nobody can go through an entire winter without one big batch of black bean soup. This soup uses the bean cooking water as its stock, which just makes the soup thicker and richer. Sautéed carrots, peppers, and onions, along with some nice cumin and chili powder, make a satisfying, colorful, and classic soup for any cold winter day or night.

Cook the beans in 9 cups of water (see Cooking Beans and Legumes, page 7). Set the beans aside without draining them.

Heat the olive oil in a stockpot over medium heat and sauté the onion, garlic, carrots, bell pepper, tomatoes, cumin, salt, and chili powder. Add 4 cups of water or stock, the tomato puree, and the cooked black beans (with their cooking liquid). After stirring, add up to 4 more cups of water or stock, depending on how thick you like your soup. Let the soup simmer for at least another 30 minutes.

THE FAMILY KITCHEN

Even kids who don't like eating beans will enjoy the fun task of picking through and sorting them. Cooking them and watching them go from hard and inedible to soft, moist, flavor-filled nuggets gives a hands-on understanding of a hard-to-explain transformation.

Creamy Wild Rice Soup ⓥ

SERVES 8 TO 12

1 ¼ cups hand-harvested and parched wild rice cooked in 3 cups water (see Wild Rice, page 70)

2 tablespoons olive oil

1 onion, chopped

2 carrots, sliced or diced

½ head celery, sliced (about 1 cup)

2 cups mushrooms (cremini or shiitake are very nice), sliced

1 tablespoon minced fresh tarragon (see Growing Green Flavor, page 64) or 2 teaspoons dried

1 tablespoon minced fresh thyme or 2 teaspoons dried

1 tablespoon minced fresh oregano or 2 teaspoons dried

2 teaspoons garlic powder

1 teaspoon salt

4 cups milk (almond or another nut milk works well for vegan version)

1 cup rice vinegar or white wine vinegar

In Minnesota, wild rice is our local "grain," even though it is actually a grass (see Wild Rice, page 70). Hand-harvested, tender wild rice is beautiful to look at, tastes delicious, and, depending upon the year, is available in many variations of gray. The more it soaks, the more the kernels open and soften. It makes flavorful soup because it becomes creamier and creamier as it cooks. It is also lovely with somewhat traditional soup flavors like celery, carrots, and savory herbs.

Heat the olive oil in a stockpot and sauté the onion, carrots, celery, and mushrooms for 5 to 7 minutes, then add the tarragon, thyme, oregano, garlic powder, and salt. Add the milk and simmer for 15 minutes. Then add the wild rice and vinegar. Simmer over low heat until the soup thickens and the rice begins to curl.

Curried Squash Soup*

SERVES 8 TO 12

2 tablespoons olive oil

1 medium yellow onion, chopped

2 cloves garlic, minced

1½ tablespoons turmeric

1½ tablespoons cumin

2 tablespoons minced fresh cilantro (see Growing Green Flavor, page 64) or 1 teaspoon ground coriander

1 tablespoon chili powder

1 tablespoon salt

1 cup apple juice

2 medium squash, peeled and roughly cubed

1 cup coconut milk plus 1 cup water or 2 cups rice milk

4 cups vegetable stock (see Making Stock, page 38) or water

3 tomatoes, diced

3 kale leaves, stemmed and chopped

Squash is a winter flavor that is simply not to be missed. Winter squash is a staple in the cold north, as it should be. It is hearty, beautiful, and nutritious. Depending on the squash, the flavor varies from as mild as potato to sweeter than carrot. The texture and colors vary too. Butternut or kabocha are my favorites for this recipe. The simplicity of the recipe and the combination of the coconut milk (if it's not obvious, one of my favorite ingredients), tomatoes, and kale make this soup close to perfect.

Heat the olive oil in a stockpot over medium heat and sauté the onion, garlic, turmeric, cumin, coriander (if using fresh cilantro, add it later with the kale), chili powder, and salt. Add the apple juice and the squash. Cover and cook until the squash is very soft, about 10 minutes. Remove the squash mixture from the pan and whisk it well or puree it in a food processor for a creamier consistency. Return the pureed squash to the pan and add the milk, stock, tomatoes, and kale. Heat through for about 10 minutes.

Winter Fish Chowder

SERVES 8 TO 12

¹/₄ cup olive oil or butter

2 leeks, rinsed and sliced

4 cloves garlic, minced

2 yams, peeled and diced

4 unpeeled potatoes, diced

4 stalks celery, sliced

1 tablespoon minced fresh basil (see Growing Green Flavor, page 64) or 2 teaspoons dried

1 tablespoon minced fresh thyme or 2 teaspoons dried

1 tablespoon minced fresh dill or 2 teaspoons dried

4 cups vegetable or fish stock (see Making Stock, page 38)

1¹/₂ pounds white fish or tilapia, cubed

¹/₄ cup pastry flour

4 cups milk of your choice

¹/₂ cup white wine

1 head broccoli, peeled and chopped

2 to 3 cups fresh or frozen corn kernels

2 teaspoons salt

2 teaspoons pepper

This chowder is an excellent way to bring fish to the table more often and add flavorful variety to the kinds of proteins you can enjoy. Here you'll find all the best parts of traditional chowder— the creamy consistency and the root vegetables—blended with delicious herbs that enhance the flavors of the fish. Enjoy this with a simple cabbage salad and whole grain bread.

Heat the olive oil in a stockpot and sauté the leeks, garlic, yams, potatoes, celery, basil, thyme, and dill. Add the stock and the fish and allow the chowder to simmer, covered, for 10 minutes. Add the flour and mix well, then add the milk and simmer for another 10 to 15 minutes. Add the wine, broccoli, corn, salt, and pepper. If the chowder is too thick for your taste, add up to 2 cups of water, as needed. Cover and simmer for about 20 minutes, or until the vegetables are tender and heated through.

THE FAMILY KITCHEN

Many kids enjoy fish, but have never seen it or handled it raw. If they are daring, let them cut the soft fish into cubes. It is important that kids who are eating meat understand something about where it comes from. Even if they do not fish, or hunt, they can learn about the creature through touching and preparing it. It can be a way of honoring the animal you are about to consume. They can also just watch, which is still a learning opportunity.

Cashew–Quinoa "Chili" ❋

SERVES 6 TO 8

1/4 cup olive oil

1 medium onion, chopped

3 cloves garlic, minced

2 unpeeled potatoes, diced

2 carrots, sliced

2 cups water

1 cup quinoa cooked in
2 cups water (see Cooking
Grains)

4 cups diced tomatoes

1 cup tomato sauce

1 tablespoon chili powder

1 tablespoon cumin

1 to 1½ tablespoons minced
fresh thyme (see Growing
Green Flavor, page 64) or
2 teaspoons dried

2 teaspoons salt

2 teaspoons garlic powder

1/4 cup maple syrup

1 cup unsalted cashews,
toasted and coarsely chopped
(see Toasting Nuts, page 27)

Once you start using quinoa, you'll discover how well it works as the grain in many recipes. This is a creative way to use the ancient grain, which is full of nutrients and is also a complete protein. The quinoa thickens the "chili," but since this soup has no beans or meat in it, it is not officially a chili at all. The cashews stand in for the beans, providing protein and a crunchy, almost legume-like texture. This satisfying stew goes well with Maple or Pumpkin Corn Bread (page 148–49) or warm tortillas.

Heat the olive oil in a stockpot over medium heat and sauté the onions and garlic. Add the potatoes, carrots, and water, cover, and simmer for 10 minutes. Add the cooked quinoa, diced tomatoes, tomato sauce, chili powder, cumin, thyme, salt, and garlic powder. Cover and simmer about 10 minutes more to allow the soup to thicken and the flavors to blend. Add the maple syrup and cashews. If the soup is too thick, add another cup of water and allow it to simmer again.

Cooking Grains

Whole grains, although not well understood, are a vital component of a healthy meal. There is more to them than whole wheat bread and oatmeal! Whole grains are full of nutrients, flavor, texture, and fiber; without them, fruits, vegetables, and proteins are nutritionally and, I believe, culinarily incomplete. Like beans, grains have enzyme inhibitors called phytates that interfere with digestion. Soaking or fermenting grains will make the nutrients most available. To do this, place grains and water in the pan they will be cooked in along with a tablespoon of vinegar or yogurt and let them sit overnight, or at least 8 hours before cooking.

When cooking grains, what you want to avoid is a mushy end product. The general rule is that 1 part grain to 2 parts water will yield around 3 parts of cooked grain. So, if you want about 3 cups of cooked grain, place 1 cup of soaked grain in a 2-quart saucepan and add 2 cups of water and $1/2$ to 1 teaspoon of salt, if desired.

Cover the saucepan and bring the water to a boil over high heat. Turn the heat down to low and simmer for the recommended cooking time. Lift the lid and test whether the grain is cooked: it should be translucent and no longer crunchy (pick up a grain and pinch it between your fingers). Do not stir the grain while you are checking it—stirring will release the starch and make the grain sticky. If the grain needs more cooking time and water is still visible around the grains, simply cover the saucepan again and simmer for another 5 to 10 minutes. If the grain needs more cooking time and all the water has been absorbed, add up to $1/4$ cup of water, cover, and continue steaming.

When the grain is tender, turn off the heat and allow the grain to rest and fluff in the steam for 5 to 10 minutes before serving. This cooking process generally works well with rice, barley, and millet as called for in my recipes.

As for rice, I always use brown rice in my recipes. There is a variety of brown rice, including short grain, long grain, and even basmati. Even though brown rice takes twice as long to cook as white rice, the nutritional content of brown rice is so superior to that of white rice (which, sadly, lacks much nutritional value at all) that I feel it is an important choice to make. It also happens to be a very kid-friendly grain because it is so sweet and chewy, so it's not such a stretch to serve it to kids. I do it all the time when I teach and, of course, at home. My friend Jean Ronnei, who directs nutrition services for St. Paul Public Schools, uses brown rice in all her rice dishes, and not only do the kids love it, they have come to expect it!

Two grains need special consideration:

- **Buckwheat** is very porous and absorbs water quickly, so bring the water to a boil and then add the buckwheat. Bring the water back to a boil, cover the pan, and then turn the heat to low and simmer until cooked.
- **Quinoa** needs to be rinsed thoroughly to get rid of a protective coating called saponin. If it's left on, the quinoa will have a bitter flavor.

The nutritional value of whole grains is not to be underestimated. Whole grains are excellent sources of B-complex vitamins, fiber, protein (quinoa is a complete protein on its own), iron, magnesium, and antioxidants, with lots of extras along the way. Millet is a great source of potassium, and brown rice contains a good deal of selenium. All of these components have the ability to reduce the effects of, for example, migraines, cancer, and heart attacks. In addition, they are important for maintaining healthy muscle and energy. Needless to say, they are a crucial part of a healthy, whole foods diet and add complexity, texture, and flavor to many dishes. I have not even delved into the depths of whole grains—there are many others I haven't included in this book that are well worth exploring. Ultimately, the most important message is that it is absolutely possible to eat grains in their natural, whole, and nutritious form without sacrificing anything. You owe it to yourself and your family to build whole grains into your food repertoire.

Miso Vegetable Soup

SERVES 6 TO 8

1 tablespoon toasted sesame oil

1 tablespoon olive oil

1 leek, rinsed and sliced

3 cloves garlic, minced

1 inch fresh ginger root, peeled and minced

2 carrots, sliced

1 winter squash, peeled and diced, or 2 zucchini, sliced

1/3 pound snap peas, trimmed (about 2 cups)

1 head broccoli, including stems, peeled and chopped (about 4 cups)

8 ounces rice noodles (wide or thin)

2/3 cup miso paste

A traditional soup from Japan, this version of miso soup includes lots of vegetables and fresh ginger sautéed in toasted sesame oil, as well as rice noodles. It is light yet very satisfying. Keep in mind that you do not want to boil this soup as that will kill the beneficial live cultures in the miso (for more about miso, see Miso–Sesame Pâté, page 1).

In a stockpot, heat the oils and sauté the leeks, garlic, ginger, carrots, and squash (zucchini will take less time than winter squash to cook, so add it later with the snap peas). Add 2 cups of water, cover, and simmer for 8 to 10 minutes, or until the squash is tender.

Meanwhile, bring 4 cups of water to a boil. Turn off the burner and add the rice noodles. Soak the noodles just until they soften, it should take only 5 to 10 minutes, and then drain them.

Add the snap peas, broccoli, and zucchini, if using, along with the drained rice noodles and an additional 10 cups of water. Remove about a cup of water from the stockpot and, using a fork or a whisk, mix the miso paste into it until it is well dissolved. Add this mixture back into the soup and simmer until heated through. Remove the soup from the heat.

THE FAMILY KITCHEN

Kids will enjoy watching the rice noodles go from crispy to soft when added to the boiling water. They will also enjoy carefully mixing the miso before returning it to the soup. Let them taste the mixture before and after adding it to see how it changes.

Spring Greens Soup with Caramelized Ramps Ⓥ

SERVES 6 TO 8

Ramps are wild leeks, but are tinged with pink and thinner than the cultivated relatives you are most likely familiar with. Their flavor is sweet with a garlicky bite—subtle and delicious. In the Midwest, if you blink in early spring, ramp season has passed. When you come upon ramps at your farmers' market or co-op, bring them home and welcome spring with this soup, which brings together other tender early-spring greens in a creamy base to support the sweet and tangy caramelized ramps.

CARAMELIZED RAMPS:

3 tablespoons olive oil

2 cups ramps, rinsed and coarsely chopped (use the entire ramp except for the very tip)

3 tablespoons maple syrup

3 tablespoons balsamic vinegar

SOUP:

3 tablespoons olive oil

2 bunches ramps, rinsed and chopped (about 2 cups)

4 cloves garlic, minced

3 tablespoons maple syrup

2 bunches greens, such as kale, collards, chard, or spinach, stemmed, and chopped into roughly 1-inch pieces

4 cups vegetable stock (see Making Stock, page 38) or water

6 cups milk (use rice milk for vegan version)

1 teaspoon salt

1 teaspoon pepper

To caramelize the ramps, heat the olive oil in a large skillet over medium heat, add the ramps, and turn the temperature down to low. Add the maple syrup and balsamic vinegar and simmer over low heat for about 30 minutes, until the liquid is thick and caramel-like. Remove the pan from the heat when all of the liquid is absorbed and the ramps are creamy and tender. Set these ramps aside for garnishing the soup.

To make the soup, heat the olive oil in a stockpot and sauté the ramps and garlic. After 3 minutes, add the maple syrup and greens, and sauté quickly. Add the stock or water. When the greens are very soft, add the milk, salt, and pepper. If you're using an immersion blender, place it in the pot and puree until the soup is very creamy and green. Otherwise, remove the pot from the heat and puree the soup in small batches in a food processor. Be sure to include greens and liquid in each batch so the soup does not spill out the bottom. Return the pureed soup to the pot and heat through. Garnish each bowl of soup with a generous helping of caramelized ramps.

THE FAMILY KITCHEN

Ramps are here for only a fleeting moment. This is a great opportunity to help kids understand seasonality as this specific soup can be prepared for only a short time. Ramps are an interesting-looking vegetable, so save a few to compare with other kinds of onions.

Carrot–Dill Soup ⓥ

SERVES 6 TO 8

3 tablespoons olive oil

1 medium onion, chopped

15 carrots, tips removed, coarsely chopped

1 tablespoon celery seed

1 teaspoon salt

1 tablespoon garlic powder

2 cups apple juice

¼ cup (about ½ bunch) finely chopped fresh dill (see Growing Green Flavor, page 64)

6 cups milk (use rice or soy milk for vegan version)

Do not dismiss or underestimate the carrot. Carrots are an incredibly versatile vegetable, so we're lucky to have them in abundance during the summer. This soup makes the most of the sweet and colorful attributes of a favorite vegetable, while the accompanying delicate dill reveals the carrot's elegance.

Heat the olive oil in a stockpot and sauté the onion, carrots, celery seed, salt, and garlic powder. Add the apple juice, cover, and simmer until the carrots are soft, about 10 minutes. Add the dill and milk. Puree the soup in small batches in a food processor and return it to the pot, or use an immersion blender to puree the soup right in the pot. Add more juice or milk to taste.

THE FAMILY KITCHEN

There is a reason that carrots are a popular baby food—kids love them! This soup makes everyone happy: It is bright and cheerful, and the dill is a familiar flavor. Let kids help with the cutting and the pureeing; however, be aware that immersion blenders can splash!

Cold Cucumber-Yogurt Soup ⓥ

SERVES 6 TO 8

5 medium cucumbers, peeled

¹⁄₄ cup (about ¹⁄₂ bunch) finely chopped fresh dill (see Growing Green Flavor, page 64)

1 cup lemon juice (about 3 medium lemons)

2 large leeks, rinsed and sliced

4 cups yogurt (or vegan alternative)

2 cups milk (or vegan alternative)

1 carrot, grated (optional)

2 to 3 large tomatoes, diced (optional)

This is a refreshing salad disguised as a delicate cold soup. It is creamy with a flavor that offers a yogurt snap. Since it can also be made without any dairy, it can be a refreshing vegan dish.

Working in batches, puree the cucumbers, dill, lemon juice, leeks, yogurt, and milk. Add water as needed to reach the desired consistency. Combine all of the batches of soup and, if desired, add the carrots or tomatoes. Refrigerate the soup until you're ready to serve.

THE FAMILY KITCHEN

Kids will giggle at the idea of soup that isn't hot. They can help with all parts of the preparation, from cutting the cucumbers to squeezing the lemon juice.

Gazpacho *

SERVES 8 TO 10

10 medium tomatoes, stemmed, seeded, and coarsely chopped

6 cloves garlic (for a fun twist, try roasting them first)

1/2 cup coarsely chopped fresh parsley or cilantro or a mix of both (see Growing Green Flavor, page 64)

2 red bell peppers, coarsely chopped (you could also use yellow peppers, or a mix of colors, but be aware that green peppers are not as sweet as red ones)

1 medium red onion, coarsely chopped

1/4 cup tamari or 2 tablespoons sea salt

2 cups apple juice or orange juice

1/2 cup lemon juice

3 or 4 stalks celery, coarsely chopped

This soup is a requirement for a full summer experience. There is nothing terribly unusual about this recipe, just fresh, seasonal ingredients. Feel free to embellish and adjust this recipe as your tastes, or your garden, permit.

Working in batches, puree all of the ingredients in a food processor. Combine the batches of soup in a large bowl and stir to combine. Make this soup your own by adding other fresh vegetables or herbs, such as cucumbers or zucchini or whatever you have in abundance. Refrigerate the soup and serve chilled.

Borscht ❧

SERVES 8 TO 12

2 tablespoons olive oil

1 large onion, sliced

4 medium potatoes, diced

8 medium beets, peeled and diced

3 tablespoons minced fresh dill (see Growing Green Flavor, page 64) or 1¹/₂ tablespoons dried

1 tablespoon caraway seed

1 tablespoon celery seed

6 cloves garlic, minced

3 large tomatoes, diced

2 teaspoons salt

10 cups water or vegetable stock (see Making Stock, page 38)

2 cups cabbage, shredded (optional)

4 medium carrots or yams, sliced thin (optional)

This is a classic soup from the Jewish and Eastern European traditions. It is delightfully deep pink and comforting. I especially like the strong dill taste combined with the hardiness of the potatoes and beets. You can also add other tubers, like yams, or squash. Borscht is traditionally served with yogurt or sour cream for a tangy taste and strong visual contrast. It is also a good soup to prepare a day ahead as it is often better the second day.

Heat the olive oil in a stockpot and sauté the onions, potatoes, and beets. Add the dill, caraway seed, celery seed, garlic, tomatoes, and salt plus 4 cups of the stock or water. Bring to a boil, and then lower the temperature and simmer, covered, until the beets and potatoes are cooked, about 20 minutes. If using other veggies, add them now along with the remaining 6 cups of water or stock. This soup gets better the longer it sits, so leave it on a low heat to simmer, covered, as long as desired, stirring occasionally. When serving, garnish each bowl of soup with a spoonful of plain yogurt, sour cream, or a vegan alternative.

THE FAMILY KITCHEN

The color of this soup is intriguing to kids. Even if they insist that they don't like beets, they will love the rich pink stew. They will also enjoy garnishing this beautiful mixture with a dollop of yogurt or sour cream, and probably steal a bite or two in the process.

New Age Potato Salad Ⓥ

SERVES 10 TO 12

8 medium red or yellow potatoes, cut into 1-inch pieces

2 cups sun-dried tomatoes softened in boiling water and cut into pieces (sun-dried tomatoes packed in oil don't need soaking)

4 tablespoons olive oil

¼ cup apple cider vinegar

1 teaspoon salt

¼ to ⅓ cup mayonnaise (use soy mayonnaise for vegan version)

2 tablespoons Dijon or stone-ground mustard

4 cloves garlic, minced

2 medium leeks or 1 bunch spring onions, rinsed and minced

¼ cup chopped fresh basil (see Growing Green Flavor, page 64) or 2 tablespoons dried

½ pound fresh spinach, stemmed and chopped

This salad takes everything good about summer and puts it all in one bowl. It has the classic heartiness of the potatoes, the richness of the sun-dried tomatoes, the depth of the fresh basil, the sweetness of the leeks, and the crispness of fresh spinach. The flavors and goodness are tied together with a pleasing dressing, and all go well with a glass of cold white wine. This is a dish that begs to be taken to a picnic.

Boil the potatoes until they're soft, then cool them immediately in cold water so they do not continue to cook and become too soft. In a large bowl, combine the potatoes, tomatoes, 2 tablespoons of the olive oil, vinegar, salt, mayonnaise, and mustard.

Heat the other 2 tablespoons of olive oil in a large skillet and sauté the garlic and leeks. When they are soft (about 3 minutes), add the basil and spinach to the pan and heat just until wilted. Remove the pan from the heat, add its contents to the potato mixture, and mix well.

THE FAMILY KITCHEN

Let the kids help with rehydrating the tomatoes. This is a great opportunity to talk about seasonal foods and the different ways of preserving them for later use. You can also talk about other dried fruits and the fact that tomatoes really are a fruit, not a vegetable. They can use a scissors to cut them into pieces. They can also help to stem the spinach and basil and cut those with a scissors too.

Garlic–Almond Kale ❦

SERVES 10 TO 12
(OR, IF YOU'RE LIKE ME,
SERVES 6)

2 tablespoons olive oil

2 tablespoons toasted sesame oil

1 large or 2 small onions, thinly sliced

3 large bunches kale, chard, mustard, or other greens, stemmed and torn into about 2-inch pieces

¹/₃ cup chopped garlic (about 12 large cloves)

¹/₄ cup tamari

1 cup toasted almonds, coarsely chopped (see Toasting Nuts, page 27)

This salad is one of the more surprising dishes that I have ever developed. It has become a Good Life signature dish. It can be served hot or cold and is delicious either way. The sautéed onions and wilted kale (or other greens as available in season) are a simple combination enhanced by the subtle flavor of toasted sesame oil. When mixed with toasted almonds and lots of lightly cooked garlic, you achieve an explosion of texture and flavor. The good nutrition becomes just a bonus.

Heat the oils in a large skillet and sauté the onion for 1 to 2 minutes over medium heat. Add the kale, garlic, tamari, and almonds and continue to sauté for another 1 to 2 minutes, until the greens are slightly wilted but bright. Remove from the heat. Serve hot or chilled.

THE FAMILY KITCHEN

The more different types of greens you use, the better. Children can rinse and drain the greens and will notice that there is a great deal of variety in leafy greens. Plus, they'll have fun tearing the greens from the stems and into bite-sized pieces.

Roasted Roots ❦

SERVES 10 TO 12

3 to 4 pounds (6 to 8 cups cut) mixed root vegetables such as beets, potatoes, carrots, and yams, scrubbed and dried

1 small winter squash

7 to 9 cloves garlic (if desired)

¼ cup olive oil

¼ cup balsamic vinegar

2 teaspoons salt

This recipe is the epitome of autumn abundance. It is fabulous on its own or combined with greens, grains, sauces, or salads. What could be more delicious and satisfying than potatoes, carrots, beets, yams, and squash caramelized in lots of olive oil and balsamic vinegar? The trick with this dish is to cut the veggies the same size and stir regularly, but not excessively, so they cook through—getting caramelized and crisp outside while remaining tender inside—without burning or sticking and crumbling. I have found that it is best to wait a while before the first turning, giving the veggies a chance to crisp and cook. After being scraped and turned once, they don't continue to stick.

Preheat the oven to 385 degrees. If your oven has a convection setting, go ahead and use it.

Peel the beets, squash, and any other vegetables you prefer peeled (I usually don't peel potatoes, carrots, and yams since their skins are full of fiber and nutrients). Cut the veggies into roughly uniform shapes, such as 1-inch cubes or long, thin wedges.

Put the cut veggies and the garlic (if using) on a baking sheet and add the olive oil, vinegar, and salt. Mix well so all the veggies are coated. Spread out the veggies so they are in a single layer and not touching, otherwise they will steam instead of roast. Roast for 25 to 30 minutes, or until tender, stirring and turning often.

THE FAMILY KITCHEN

If you cut them long and thin like French fries, kids are more excited to eat these vegetables; the color and sweetness also motivate kids to try them. If it appeals to them, let them dip the "fries" in ketchup, mustard, or mayo.

Golden Pecan–Rice Salad ❦

SERVES 10 TO 12

8 tablespoons olive oil

6 cloves garlic, minced

1 medium yam, peeled, or 2 large carrots, thinly sliced

2 medium gold beets, peeled, halved, and sliced thinly

¹/₄ cup water

1 large (about 6 inches long) or 2 small zucchini or yellow squash, sliced

2 cups brown rice cooked in 4 cups water (see Cooking Grains, page 48)

¹/₃ cup fruity balsamic vinegar or white balsamic vinegar

1 teaspoon celery seed

1 tablespoon minced fresh thyme (see Growing Green Flavor, page 64) or 2 teaspoons dried

1 teaspoon salt

1 cup pecans, toasted and coarsely chopped (see Toasting Nuts, page 27)

The yellows and oranges of the beets, squash, and carrots lend this salad visual beauty and lots of flavor. The pecans take the taste one step further. I love to use nuts in any way that I can. If you can find peach (or any other fruity) balsamic vinegar, it adds a lovely touch. The whole combination is a winner.

Heat 2 tablespoons of the olive oil in a heavy skillet and sauté the garlic, yams, and beets over medium heat for 3 minutes. Add the water, cover, and cook over a low heat until just soft, about 8 minutes. Add the zucchini, cover the pan again, and continue cooking for another 2 to 3 minutes. When the vegetables are soft (not mushy), transfer them to a large bowl. Add the cooked rice and stir to combine.

In a small bowl, whisk together the remaining 6 tablespoons of olive oil, vinegar, celery seed, thyme, and salt, then pour the dressing over the rice and vegetable mixture. Add the toasted pecans. Mix well.

This dish can be served warm, at room temperature, or cold. It also stores well in the refrigerator, so it works well as a make-ahead dish.

THE FAMILY KITCHEN

Here's a recipe that helps younger children learn that a vegetable can have many varieties—beets aren't just garnet colored. Each family member can have a role in preparing this recipe, from peeling and chopping up the vegetables to giving careful and constant attention to the nuts as they toast (with adult assistance) to pouring the vinegar and sprinkling the herbs.

Luscious Lima Bean Salad *

SERVES 8 TO 10

SALAD:

2 cups lima beans

2 medium butternut squash peeled and diced into 1/2-inch cubes

10 cloves garlic, peeled

Olive oil for roasting and sautéing (about 2 tablespoons total)

3 red bell peppers

2 leeks, rinsed and thinly sliced

DRESSING:

1/3 cup olive oil

1/2 cup raspberry vinegar

1 tablespoon minced fresh thyme (see Growing Green Flavor, page 64) or 1 1/2 teaspoons dried

1 tablespoon cumin

2 teaspoons celery seed

2 teaspoons salt

Soft butternut squash and big tender lima beans are enough all by themselves. Add roasted garlic and red peppers as well as sweet sautéed leeks and raspberry vinegar, and the colors alone will bring you happiness. This dish has all the elements of late autumn comfort food.

Cook the lima beans in 5 cups of water (see Cooking Beans and Legumes, page 7) and set them aside to cool. Steam the squash in a vegetable steamer or boil it in 2 cups of water until it's soft (about 8 minutes), drain, and set aside.

Preheat the oven to 400 degrees. Mix the garlic with a tablespoon of olive oil in a small dish and bake for 15 to 20 minutes. Set it aside. Brush the peppers with olive oil and roast them in the oven until they're charred on the outside, about 25 to 30 minutes. You can also roast the peppers over an open flame, but when doing so, do not brush the peppers with oil. Hold the peppers with tongs about an inch from the open flame and turn them so they are evenly charred, about 2 minutes per side. Place the roasted peppers in a paper bag and let them cool. This steams the peppers so the skins come off easily. When they have cooled completely, peel off the skin, cut out the stem and seeds, and chop them into half-inch squares.

Heat a tablespoon of olive oil in a heavy skillet over a medium flame and sauté the leeks until they're soft, about 3 minutes. Combine the lima beans, squash, garlic, peppers, and leeks in a large bowl and mix well.

For the dressing, whisk together the olive oil, vinegar, thyme, cumin, celery seed, and salt in a small bowl. Pour the dressing over the vegetables and mix well.

Quinoa and White Beans with Raspberry Dressing ⓥ

SERVES 6 TO 8

SALAD:

1½ cups navy or other dried white beans cooked in 4 cups water (see Cooking Beans and Legumes, page 7)

1 cup quinoa cooked in 2 cups water (see Cooking Grains, page 48)

1 small red onion, sliced thinly

1 pound mixed salad greens

4 ounces feta cheese, crumbled (omit for vegan version)

DRESSING:

1 cup raspberries

½ cup apple cider vinegar

2 tablespoons honey (use agave syrup for vegan version)

¼ cup water

1 teaspoon salt

¼ cup mayonnaise (use soy mayonnaise for vegan version)

2 cloves garlic, minced

¼ cup olive oil

1 teaspoon minced fresh tarragon (see Growing Green Flavor, page 64)

2 teaspoons crushed fresh thyme

Quinoa is a fantastic addition to the whole grain repertoire. It is an ancient grain that has become popular in the natural foods community—for good reason. Being a complete protein, quinoa is highly nutritious. It cooks quickly, in about 15 minutes. And, this incredibly versatile grain is delicious with beans, tofu, chicken, meat, or fish and with spicy, tangy, sweet, or herby flavoring.

Bring the raspberries, vinegar, honey, and water to a boil over medium heat. Reduce the heat and simmer for 15 to 20 minutes. Let the raspberry mixture cool. Add the salt, mayonnaise, garlic, olive oil, tarragon, and thyme. Mix well.

Combine the beans, quinoa, onions, and salad greens in a bowl. Dress the salad lightly, tossing to combine the ingredients. Top the salad with crumbled feta.

THE FAMILY KITCHEN

Kids love fresh berries. They will enjoy stirring and mixing the dressing ingredients in this recipe and watching as the color changes to bright pink.

Rosemary Chicken Salad

SERVES 8 TO 10

CHICKEN:

2 pounds (4 to 5) boneless chicken breasts

2 cloves garlic, peeled and slice in half lengthwise

Olive oil

Salt

SALAD:

1 bunch green onions, minced

4 cloves garlic, minced

1/2 cup walnuts, chopped

1/4 cup fresh rosemary, minced (see Growing Green Flavor, page 64)

2 tablespoons olive oil

2 tablespoons white wine vinegar

1/3 cup mayonnaise

1 teaspoon salt

Rosemary and chicken are natural companions. This salad highlights these flavors, which are complemented by the subtle tartness of white wine vinegar and the added crunch of walnuts. Rosemary is one of the most fragrant and beautiful herbs to keep growing on a window ledge (see Growing Green Flavor, page 64).

Preheat the oven to 350 degrees. Rub the chicken breasts with the cut side of the garlic, a dash of salt, and about a tablespoon of olive oil and place them in a roasting pan. Bake the chicken breasts for 20 to 25 minutes or until the juices run clear. (Try cooking the breasts on the grill for a flavor twist.) Allow the chicken to cool, then slice or chop it into smaller, bite-sized pieces.

Combine the chopped chicken with the onions, minced garlic, walnuts, rosemary, olive oil, vinegar, mayonnaise, and salt. Mix well.

Growing Green Flavor

*P*art of the wonder and enjoyment of cooking with locally produced goods is becoming aware of the seasonality of food. Spring is certain when you sauté the first stalks of asparagus. In late summer you relish the flavor of a vine-ripened tomato the most, knowing that it might be the last. Autumn is even more golden with the sweet flavor of a roasted butternut squash. And winter's chill is easier to tolerate when relieved with a hearty potato stew.

There is one part of cooking up the good life that can offer year-round freshness: herbs. Fresh herbs are superior in flavor and nutrition to their dried remnants. With little fuss, you can have an abundant supply of basil, bay leaf, cilantro (and coriander), chives, garlic chives, lemon grass, marjoram, mint, oregano, rosemary, sage, and thyme by growing them indoors.

With a minimal investment in small plants or seed, you can explore the different varieties—sometimes subtle—within many cultivars. For example, basil comes in a multitude of varieties: cinnamon, lemon, lettuce leaf, licorice, opal, purple ruffles, spicy globe, sweet, and Thai. Mint offers another world of culinary flavor, and in

basil

addition to the traditional peppermint and spearmint, can be had in the more exotic apple, bergamot (or orange), chocolate, Corsican, Egyptian, ginger, Persian, and pineapple. Keep your mint plants separate so their flavors stay true and strong. In addition to the soft gray-green of garden sage, try the golden or berggarten varieties. And definitely go beyond the comfort zone of curled parsley (as a ubiquitous afterthought on a diner's plate, a cutting of parsley on your plate used to mean that the master chef had personally prepared your order). Grow the more flavorful flat-leafed parsley varieties, called Italian or plain Italian dark green.

Be creative with your definition of *container* and look beyond the traditional clay pot on the windowsill. Fill a hanging basket with mint and hang it in a sunny window in the bathroom. Or cultivate rosemary in an old water pitcher with a broken handle. As a rule, containers around ten inches in diameter and at least four inches deep work well, although a depth of twelve to fifteen inches will allow your basil, chives, and mint more root space for longer and better growth. And with the exception of keeping mint to itself, you can experiment with growing two or more varieties together in a larger pot.

Whatever the container, make certain you provide the plants with good drainage. Put about an inch of small stones or gravel at the bottom of the container. Drain holes at the bottom are fine, but it's even better for the plants' roots if the container has holes every two or three inches around its lower edge, about a quarter inch to a half inch up from the bottom.

Fill the prepared container with a good potting soil mix. That means do not use garden soil; it's too heavy. Ready-made mixes for indoor growing are inexpensive and of good quality.

Follow the instructions for seeding provided on the seed packet. A good rule of (green?) thumb is to plant seeds to a depth of about three times the diameter of the seed. You can go ahead and mess around with planting in starter pots and transplanting, but it's really not necessary if you're careful to spread the seeds out sufficiently. Thin the seedlings as they emerge so the remaining plants will have room to grow strong.

mint

Keep the plants in as much sun possible; good lighting is critical to productive growth. A southwest window is ideal. During the darker months of winter,

rosemary

your herbs will be less productive, so scale back on cutting and use. If you want, you can go the route of supplemental lighting, but if you are not interested or able to devote that much serious time to herb growing, let the plants run their cycle. If the leaves start dropping and the plants seem tired, let them rest, or even die out—and don't feel guilty. The plant is just running its life course, so growing herbs is another aspect of understanding the seasonality of edibles. It's easy to either reseed or start with another small plant.

Annuals such as cilantro do not come back after they go to seed and die, so you will need to reseed to produce a continuous crop. Try having three containers at different growth stages: seeded, intermediate, and ready to cut and use.

As you harvest your herbs, pinch and trim the leaves and stems you need from the top of the plant first. This will help keep the plant from getting leggy and encourage new growth along the stems of the plant.

With enough sun and a little water (don't overdo it—water the plants only when the soil feels dry to the touch), your herbs will thrive and be ready to add even more flavor to your good life.

Mediterranean Millet "Couscous" Ⓥ

2¹/₂ cups millet

2 tablespoons olive oil

1 large onion, thinly sliced

6 cloves garlic, chopped

12 sun-dried tomatoes, softened in boiling water and cut into strips (sun-dried tomatoes packed in oil don't need soaking)

1 tablespoon cumin

¹/₄ cup lemon juice

1 tablespoon chopped fresh basil (see Growing Green Flavor, page 64) or 2 teaspoons dried

1 teaspoon salt

¹/₄ cup balsamic vinegar

1¹/₂ cups chopped spinach

1 cup pitted olives, coarsely chopped

¹/₂ pound crumbled feta (omit for vegan version)

¹/₂ cup toasted pine nuts (optional)

Couscous is a delicious type of pasta, but my favorite thing about this salad is that it uses millet instead of couscous. Millet is a nonglutinous grain that is high in protein, fiber, vitamins, and minerals. It offers a subtle sweetness that will keep anyone from even noticing that it's not couscous. The richness of the ingredients make this salad feel like an extravagance, but the sun-dried tomatoes, pine nuts, feta cheese, and spinach are now all familiar ingredients. You can choose your favorite olives (I like Greek Kalamata or Italian Saracen varieties). The combination of lemon and balsamic vinegar creates a particularly unusual tang, and with the addition of good extra-virgin olive oil, you get the true taste of the Mediterranean. This is a nice dish to serve warm, at room temperature, or even as a cold salad, although it is substantial enough to be a main course.

Cook the millet in 5 cups of water (see Cooking Grains, page 48). Fluff the cooked millet with a fork to prevent clumps. Put the millet in a bowl and set it aside to cool.

Heat the olive oil in a heavy skillet over medium heat and sauté the onion, garlic, tomatoes, and cumin. Add the lemon juice, basil, salt, and vinegar. Cook until the flavors are well blended and the vegetables are soft, about 5 to 7 minutes. Add the spinach and cook just long enough to wilt it, about 30 seconds. Combine the sautéed mixture with the fluffed and cooled millet and toss with the olives, feta, and pine nuts.

Note: I sometimes substitute peeled and sliced eggplant or sliced peppers for the spinach in this recipe. If you do this, sauté these denser vegetables separately in 2 tablespoons of olive oil for 3 to 5 minutes before adding them to the salad.

THE FAMILY KITCHEN

Kids can enjoy cutting the olives and rehydrated sun-dried tomatoes and fluffing the millet. This is a great opportunity to talk about the difference between couscous (a pasta) and millet (a whole grain).

Sesame-Ginger Soba Noodles ❋

SERVES 6 TO 8

2 pounds soba noodles

2 tablespoons toasted sesame oil or coconut oil

4 cups mixed chopped vegetables such as leeks, carrots, broccoli, and bell peppers

SAUCE:

2 inches fresh ginger, peeled and coarsely chopped

¹/₂ cup miso paste

¹/₄ cup maple syrup

¹/₂ cup toasted sesame oil

2 cups tahini

2 teaspoons salt

¹/₂ cup lemon juice

1¹/₂ cups apple juice

1¹/₂ cups water (or as much as needed for desired consistency)

Soba noodles, a lovely, light, whole grain buckwheat noodle, are a great alternative to typical semolina pasta. They are usually a blend of whole wheat and buckwheat, but it is possible to find 100 percent buckwheat noodles. You can also use rice noodles with this dish. Soba are typically used in Asian cooking, so an Asian-style sauce is perfect. This sauce has a nice blend of fresh ginger, toasted sesame oil, and lemon juice. It has a sweetness that actually enhances the ginger and sesame flavors and makes people want to scrape the bowl you mixed it in. Add sautéed vegetables and tofu, or mock duck or chicken, for a delightful, light, and flavorful meal.

Cook the soba noodles as instructed on the package. These noodles cook quickly and can become sticky if overcooked, so drain them immediately when cooked and cool them under cold water. Set aside.

In a large skillet, heat 2 tablespoons of oil over medium heat and sauté the vegetables. Set them aside.

Chop the ginger in a food processor, then add the miso, maple syrup, sesame oil, tahini, and salt and puree, slowly adding the juice and water to the running machine until the sauce reaches the desired consistency. In a large bowl, combine the noodles and vegetables with the sauce.

Black Bean, Tofu, and Miso Salad *

SERVES 10 TO 12

4 cups dried black beans

2 pounds extra-firm tofu, cut into 1-inch cubes

4 tablespoons oil

3 red bell peppers, diced

2 bunches green onions or 1 large leek, rinsed and sliced

¹/₂ cup miso paste

1¹/₂ cups rice vinegar

1 tablespoon red pepper flakes (if you are concerned about spiciness, leave these out and add them at the table)

I never would have thought that black turtle beans and miso made sense, but then I thought of Asian fermented black beans. This dish is like a cousin (for more about miso, see Miso–Sesame Pâté, page 1). This salad uses tofu as well, so it is high in protein, and its relative blandness handles the strong miso, rice vinegar, and red pepper flavors nicely. Green onions and sweet peppers finish it off.

Cook the beans in 10 cups of water until tender (see Cooking Beans and Legumes, page 7). Rinse the beans and let them cool.

Meanwhile, fry the tofu in the oil until it's nicely browned on all sides. Combine the tofu with the beans and add the peppers and green onions.

Mix the miso paste, rice vinegar, and red pepper flakes. Dress the bean mixture with the miso sauce and stir to combine.

Tangy Cashew Wild Rice ❧

SERVES 10 TO 12

1½ cups hand-parched wild rice cooked in 3 cups water (see Wild Rice, page 70)

1½ cups brown rice cooked in 3 cups water (see Cooking Grains, page 48)

2 yams, peeled and diced into 1-inch pieces

2 tablespoons toasted sesame oil

2 tablespoons olive oil

2 leeks, rinsed and sliced thinly on the diagonal

4 stalks celery, sliced thinly on the diagonal

2 medium red bell peppers, sliced into thin strips (optional)

1 cup toasted cashews or other nuts (see Toasting Nuts, page 27)

1 cup dried apricots, chopped

DRESSING:

2 tablespoons olive oil

2 tablespoons toasted sesame oil

1½ tablespoons celery seed

1½ tablespoons chili powder

1½ tablespoons garlic powder

⅓ cup cider vinegar

2 teaspoons salt

This salad of brown rice and wild rice mixed with leeks, celery, yams, and red peppers offers a colorful and savory combination. After you add the cashews, apricots, and celery seed, the result is a mixture of sweet and crunchy that is at once familiar and surprising with its hard-to-identify and delightful spices. This salad has pretty much everything you could want.

While the cooked rice cools, steam the yams until tender in a vegetable steamer set over water.

Heat the oils in a large, heavy skillet and sauté the leeks, celery, peppers, and steamed yams.

In a small bowl, mix together the dressing ingredients. Combine the sautéed vegetables with the rice and add the toasted nuts and chopped apricots. Pour the dressing over the rice and vegetable combination and mix thoroughly.

This dish can be served warm, at room temperature, or cold. It keeps well in the refrigerator.

THE FAMILY KITCHEN

Turkish dried apricots are most common, but domestically grown and dried apricots from California are sweeter. At the market you might want to buy a few of each and make your own taste comparison. Use the unsulfured version—they are not bright orange like the sulfured type, but don't contain any dangerous sulfites and taste identical.

Wild Rice

Wild rice is in a category by itself. Although it is Minnesota's state grain, it is not rice at all, but a grass. Wild rice is considered a sacred gift by the Ojibwe people. The grain, which ranges from dark gray to light gray to chocolate in color, is rich in protein and the amino acid lysine, among other nutrients.

Do not confuse real wild rice, called manoomin by the Ojibwe, with its genetic cousin commonly sold in grocery stores. That is a hybrid, developed at the University of Minnesota. During recent years, there has been some controversy over the way wild rice should be bred and grown, but controversy aside, the hybrid cousin bears a closer resemblance to broken black needles than to food. This "wild" rice is cultivated in paddies, harvested by combines, cooks uniformly, and is consistently the same year after year. Although it is substantially less expensive than its original ancestor, it is not cheap.

True wild rice is not cultivated, but grows naturally in lakes throughout northern Minnesota and nearby Canada. Each year the size of the wild rice crop will depend upon seasonal conditions. The wild rice plants thrive in rich lake bottoms and shallow rivers, which are full of nutrients, in places where summers are filled with warm days and cool nights. In the autumn, the wild rice is hand harvested and hand parched by Anishinaabe Ojibwe using traditionally based methods. There will be two people to a canoe, with one person poling the canoe through the rice bed while the other knocks the rice off the stems with sticks. The harvested rice is then taken to a rice mill for finishing. First the rice is toasted, or parched, a few hundred pounds at a time in iron barrels over a wood fire. The rice is constantly turned to prevent burning. The parched wild rice is cooled and then jigged and winnowed: a thrashing machine takes off the outer hull and then a fanning mill separates the hulls from the rice.

There are a few traditional finishers of wild rice in Minnesota, and one of the leaders in preserving this culinary gem is the White Earth Land Recovery Project. Founded by Winona LaDuke, White Earth Land Recovery Project received the International Slow Food Award for the Defense of Biodiversity in 2003.

It is crucial both to the sustainability of the land and of Native American culture that we understand the distinctions between types of wild rice and that we support the people protecting and maintaining this traditional food.

As described, true wild rice does not resemble the cultivated variety and is markedly lighter in appearance. In fact, depending on the growing conditions from year to year, natural wild rice can range from soft grey to rich milk chocolate in color. It pops open completely when cooked and is soft and tender to eat. Once you have savored this version, the other kind will never again suffice.

Three Methods for Cooking Wild Rice

1 cup hand-parched wild rice, well rinsed
3 cups water
1 teaspoon salt

Stove Top
Combine the rice, water, and salt in a saucepan, cover it, and bring to a boil over medium heat. Some hand-parched rice will only take 15 to 20 minutes to cook, so check to see if it is tender and has fluffed open. Drain any excess water.

Oven
Combine the rice, water, and salt in a covered baking dish and bake at 350 degrees for 1 hour. Check the rice an hour into baking to see if the water is absorbed and the rice has fluffed open. If not, continue baking for another 30 to 40 minutes.

Microwave
Combine the rice, water, and salt in a 3-quart glass casserole, cover, and microwave on high for 6 minutes. Then microwave on low (or the defrost setting) for 20 minutes. Remove from the microwave and let sit covered for 10 to 15 minutes.

Herbed Yam and Potato Salad ⓥ

SERVES 10 TO 12

4 medium yams, peeled and cut into 1-inch cubes

6 to 8 medium potatoes, cut into 1-inch cubes

⅓ cup olive oil

⅓ cup raspberry vinegar

⅓ cup mayonnaise (use soy mayonnaise for vegan version)

2 teaspoons salt

1 tablespoon garlic powder

¼ cup fresh rosemary (see Growing Green Flavor, page 64), minced, or 1 tablespoon dried

½ cup fresh basil, chopped, or 2 tablespoons dried

¼ cup minced fresh thyme or 1 tablespoon dried

4 stalks celery, diced

1 leek or 2 green onions, rinsed and diced

One of the joys of cooking is turning something familiar into something different. This recipe is the result of experimenting with traditional potato salad. The addition of yams brings a fresh twist, and the raspberry vinegar enhances their sweetness.

Boil the yams and potatoes until soft. Remove from the heat, drain, and cool under cold water. While the yams and potatoes are cooling, mix the olive oil, vinegar, mayonnaise, salt, garlic powder, rosemary, basil, thyme, celery, and leeks in a large bowl. Add the cooled yams and potatoes to the bowl and stir to combine.

Latin "Couscous"

SERVES 6 TO 8

1 cup millet

1 cup quinoa

1 bunch green onions, chopped

4 cloves garlic, minced

1 red bell pepper, minced

2 cups fresh or frozen corn kernels

2 cups fresh or frozen shelled edamame (green soybeans), steamed

1 ripe avocado, peeled and diced

DRESSING:

1 large fresh tomato or 1/3 cup tomato juice

1/3 cup olive oil

2 tablespoons maple syrup

2 tablespoons Dijon mustard

1/4 cup champagne or white wine vinegar

1/4 cup sherry vinegar

1/2 cup (about 1/2 bunch) minced fresh cilantro (see Growing Green Flavor, page 64)

1 teaspoon cumin

1 teaspoon salt

Millet and quinoa take the place of the pasta couscous in this recipe. The millet and quinoa taste as good as, if not better than, couscous, but carry a load of fiber and nutrients that couscous can't match. The savory tomato dressing brings an exotic Latin dance step to the flavor, and the corn, edamame, and avocadoes definitely place this recipe south of the border in taste. It is light, full of flavor, and works well at a picnic or as a side to your favorite grilled meat.

Place the millet and 4 cups of water in a large pan with a tight-fitting lid. Bring to a boil, cover, reduce to a simmer, and cook for 10 minutes. Then add the quinoa to the pot and simmer, covered, for another 15 minutes. Allow the grains to cool in a bowl. When cooled, add the onions, garlic, red pepper, corn, edamame, and avocado.

To make the dressing, quarter the fresh tomato and use a fork to scrape the pulp into a small bowl. It's fine to leave in a few seeds. (And toss the skins into your accumulating vegetable stock store. See Making Stock, page 38.) Whisk the tomato pulp together with the olive oil, maple syrup, mustard, vinegar, cilantro, cumin, and salt. Pour the dressing over the salad and stir to combine.

THE FAMILY KITCHEN

Kids will enjoy mixing the dressing and pouring it onto the salad. They can also help remove the edamame from the pods (though you can also buy these already shelled) and cutting the soft avocado.

Brussels Sprouts with Honey–Horseradish Sauce Ⓥ

SERVES 8 TO 10

1 pound Brussels sprouts, halved

3 medium sweet potatoes, peeled and sliced thinly

2 leeks, rinsed and sliced thinly

6 tablespoons olive oil

¼ cup prepared mustard

¼ cup prepared horseradish

⅔ cup honey (use ½ cup apple or orange juice for vegan version)

¼ cup cider vinegar

4 cloves garlic, minced

1 inch ginger, peeled and minced

½ teaspoon salt

Brussels sprouts intrigued me as a kid. We only had them once or twice a year, but they were like fun little mini cabbages—slightly bitter and light and leafy at the same time. This sauce is what makes them work here. The Brussels sprouts combine with the mellow flavor of the sweet potatoes for a beautiful balance of bitter and sweet.

Preheat the oven to 385 degrees. In a large baking pan, toss the Brussels sprouts, sweet potatoes, and leeks with 2 tablespoons of the olive oil until the veggies are well coated. Roast for about 20 minutes, until the vegetables are tender and brightly colored.

Meanwhile, combine the remaining ¼ cup of olive oil, mustard, horseradish, honey, vinegar, garlic, ginger, and salt in a medium bowl. Add the roasted vegetables to the bowl and stir gently until all the veggies are coated in the sauce.

Rainbow Rice

SERVES 8 TO 10

3 pounds beets

1 medium red onion, sliced

2 medium red bell peppers, sliced

3 medium tomatoes, diced

6 cloves garlic, finely chopped

5 tablespoons olive oil

2 tablespoons fresh dill (see Growing Green Flavor, page 64) or 1 tablespoon dried

2 teaspoons celery seed

2 teaspoons salt

2/3 cup balsamic vinegar

1¹/₂ cups brown rice cooked in 3 cups water (see Cooking Grains, page 48)

1¹/₂ cups wild rice cooked in 3 cups water (see Wild Rice, page 70)

This colorful and sweet combination offers a new way to eat beets. With the rice and the sweet peppers, and with the strength of the dill, this salad is a celebration of spring, almost like a salad version of borscht, and it tastes even better than it looks.

Boil the beets whole, let them cool, and then peel and slice them. Lightly sauté the onion, peppers, tomatoes, and garlic in 1 tablespoon of olive oil. Stir in the dill, celery seed, salt, vinegar, and remaining 4 tablespoons of olive oil. In a large bowl, combine the beets, wild and brown rice, and sauté mixture. Mix well.

Polenta and Artichoke Salad ✤

SERVES 6 TO 8

3 cups water

1 teaspoon salt

1¹/₂ cups polenta or coarse cornmeal

¹/₃ cup olive oil, plus 2–3 tablespoons additional for frying polenta

¹/₃ cup balsamic vinegar

¹/₄ cup lemon juice

4 cloves garlic, minced

1 teaspoon salt

1 small red onion, sliced thinly

2 (14-ounce) cans (about 2¹/₂ to 3 cups) artichoke hearts, finely chopped or pureed

2 cups sun-dried tomatoes, rehydrated in warm water and chopped or cut with scissors

1 cup capers

This dish began as an accidental discovery during an attempt to use up leftover polenta. The delicious dense grain of polenta combined with the tangy lemon and the artichokes, tomatoes, and capers results in a savory, multilayered, and well-balanced salad. The combination is really lip smacking.

Bring the salted water to a boil, then slowly add the polenta, whisking regularly to remove lumps. Simmer the mixture and continue stirring it for about 5 minutes. Remove the polenta from the heat and pour it into an oiled 9 × 13-inch pan. Spread it so it is about a half inch thick. When the polenta is cool, cut it into 1-inch pieces.

While the polenta cools, make the dressing. Whisk together the ¹/₃ cup of olive oil, vinegar, and lemon juice and then add the garlic and salt. Set aside.

Fry the polenta pieces in 2 to 3 tablespoons of olive oil until well browned on both sides. Transfer the fried polenta to a bowl, add the onion, artichokes, sun-dried tomatoes, and capers, and toss with the dressing.

Note: If you eat meat, you'll find that a pound of cooked and diced chicken breast makes a great addition to this dish.

THE FAMILY KITCHEN

Kids will enjoy cutting the cooked and cooled soft polenta with a butter knife. Or give them small cookie cutters and let them get creative with shapes! The artichokes are also an unusual vegetable that kids can enjoy crushing with a fork.

Asparagus and Artichoke Pasta Ⓥ

SERVES 8 TO 10

1/4 cup olive oil

1 medium onion, sliced

1 bunch (about a pound) asparagus, ends removed (see The Family Kitchen) and cut into 2-inch pieces

6 cups whole grain pasta cooked in 10 cups water

DRESSING:

2 cups canned artichoke hearts

3 cloves garlic

1/4 cup lemon juice

1/3 cup balsamic vinegar

1/2 cup capers, rinsed and drained

1 teaspoon salt

Asiago or Parmesan to taste (omit for vegan version)

Asparagus season is fleeting, so you want to serve asparagus as often as you can while it's available. Find the most tender stalks and pair them with artichoke for a truly fresh spring flavor. The artichoke dressing is light with citrus, and the capers add small bursts of flavor. The asparagus is not covered up in a heavy sauce with this recipe, so it gets the full attention it deserves.

In a large skillet, heat the olive oil and sauté the onion and asparagus until the asparagus is bright green. Combine the veggies in a bowl with the cooked pasta.

To make the dressing, puree the artichoke hearts, garlic, and lemon juice in a food processor. Scrape the puree into a small bowl and stir in the vinegar, capers, and salt. Pour the dressing over the pasta and artichoke combination and top with grated Asiago or Parmesan cheese (if using).

THE FAMILY KITCHEN

I prefer to break off the woody ends of asparagus stalks rather than cut them. Just bend the end of the stalk until it snaps. Sometimes you'll break off less than a fourth of the stalk, and sometimes more, but the stalk will break where it begins to get tough and stringy. Discard the bottom part of the stem. Because breaking the ends of asparagus is intuitive, kids can really get this one. It's all in the touch. Just tell them to close their eyes and feel for the spot where it wants to break. More often than not it will be just the right spot!

Asparagus with Citrus and Olive Marinade ⓥ

SERVES 8 TO 10

MARINADE:

Juice of 1/2 lemon (about 3 tablespoons)

2 tablespoons honey (use agave syrup for vegan version)

1/4 cup olive oil

1/4 cup champagne vinegar

2 teaspoons salt

4 cloves garlic, minced

2 tablespoons minced fresh thyme (see Growing Green Flavor, page 64) or 2 teaspoons dried

2 very ripe navel oranges or tangerines, peeled, seeded, and coarsely chopped with their juice

1 cup Kalamata olives, pitted and chopped

ASPARAGUS:

1/4 cup water

2 tablespoons olive oil

2 pounds asparagus, trimmed (see The Family Kitchen, page 76) and cut in thirds

1/2 red onion, sliced very thinly

The combination of lemon and orange with the Mediterranean olives is fantastic. Although the flavors are strong, they enhance the freshness and spring feeling of this marinade. Add the slightly bitter, melt-in-your-mouth tenderness of fresh local asparagus for a unique, tangy taste of the season.

Prepare the marinade by combining the lemon juice, honey, 1/4 cup of olive oil, vinegar, salt, garlic, and thyme and whisk well. Stir in the oranges with their juice and the olives and set aside.

In a saucepan, heat the water and 2 tablespoons of olive oil. When almost boiling, place the asparagus and red onion in the pan, cover, and steam until the asparagus is bright green and tender, about 2 to 3 minutes. Remove the onions and asparagus from the pan and cover with the marinade. Chill for up to 4 hours.

THE FAMILY KITCHEN

In addition to breaking the woody ends off the asparagus, kids can help peel and chop the citrus and squeeze the juice. They will enjoy the sweet and tangy smell and the sticky juice on their hands, especially if they can lick it off.

Early Greens with Miso Dressing and Toasted Almonds ❋

SERVES 8 TO 10

GREENS:

2 tablespoons olive oil

2 tablespoons toasted sesame oil

2 medium onions or 2 leeks, sliced

6 cloves garlic, minced

1 inch ginger, peeled and minced

2 pounds assorted greens (such as arugula, mustard, or spinach), well rinsed and dried

2 cups sliced or crushed almonds, toasted (see Toasting Nuts, page 27)

MISO DRESSING:

1/3 cup rice vinegar

2 tablespoons honey or maple syrup (use the maple syrup for a vegan version)

2 tablespoons stone-ground mustard

1/2 cup miso paste

2 tablespoons toasted sesame oil

1/3 cup olive oil

2 teaspoons tamari

This is the recipe that I use in cooking classes to prove that I can get anyone to eat leafy greens. People love this combination of sweet, spicy, savory, and sour. The toasted sesame oil is balanced by the rice vinegar, which is complemented by the miso (read more about miso in Miso–Sesame Pâté, page 1), and tempered by the maple syrup, which works perfectly with the mustard. All of it is topped off with the crunch and flavor of the almonds. The dressing also is delicious on just about any vegetable and even on proteins like tofu and fish.

In a saucepan, heat the oils over medium heat, add the onions and sauté until soft, 2 to 3 minutes, then add the garlic and ginger. Add the greens handful by handful, stirring constantly. Sauté until all the greens are added and have wilted into a bright green, about 2 minutes. Remove immediately from heat and place in a large bowl. Allow the mixture to cool before adding the toasted almonds.

To make the dressing, whisk together the vinegar, honey, mustard, miso paste, sesame oil, olive oil, and tamari in a small bowl. Pour the dressing over the greens and toss to mix.

THE FAMILY KITCHEN

Crushing almonds can be fun. You don't need to use a knife at all. My favorite way to do it is under the bottom of a jar. So far it is the most efficient method I have found for crushing toasted nuts. Kids can also use a rolling pin.

Israeli Couscous

SERVES 10 TO 12

3 cups Israeli couscous

2 pints grape tomatoes

6 tablespoons olive oil

1½ teaspoons salt

2 leeks or 1 bunch ramps or green onions, rinsed and chopped

4 cloves garlic, minced

¼ cup coarsely chopped fresh basil (see Growing Green Flavor, page 64) or 2 tablespoons dried

2 tablespoons minced fresh thyme or 1 teaspoon dried

Juice of 1 lemon

1 cup Greek or Mediterranean olives, pitted and coarsely chopped

½ cup feta, crumbled

Israeli couscous is visually intriguing, and has more texture and density than traditional couscous. Look for the large kind at specialty groceries and at co-ops. While Israeli couscous is a fun variation, regular couscous can be used in this recipe too.

Soak the couscous in 6 cups of boiling water for 45 minutes and then set it aside.

Preheat the oven to 400 degrees. Slice the tomatoes in half, place them in a baking pan, and drizzle them with 3 tablespoons of the olive oil and 1 teaspoon of the salt. Roast the tomatoes for about 20 minutes, until the tomatoes are shriveled but still moist. Set them aside.

In a large skillet, heat the remaining 3 tablespoons of olive oil over medium heat and sauté the leeks until they just turn translucent, then add the garlic, basil, thyme, and lemon juice. Remove the pan from the heat and add the olives, remaining ½ teaspoon of salt, and tomatoes. Let the mixture cool and then combine it with the cooked couscous. Top with the feta cheese just before serving.

THE FAMILY KITCHEN

The actual couscous is so interesting that kids will simply enjoy just preparing it. Seeing it in this dish may be compelling enough for them to give it a try—or else they can try it plain with butter and parmesan cheese.

Marinated Veggies

SERVES 10 TO 12

12 cups assorted vegetables (such as 1 head broccoli, 1 head cauliflower, 4 carrots, 2 zucchini, ½ pound green beans, and 2 red bell peppers—whatever is in seasonal abundance)

1 cup pitted, minced olives (optional)

1 cup cherry tomatoes (optional)

MARINADE:

1 cup olive oil

½ cup balsamic vinegar

½ cup raspberry or apple cider vinegar

3 tablespoons maple syrup

3 tablespoons stone-ground mustard

2 tablespoons minced fresh thyme (see Growing Green Flavor, page 64) or 2 teaspoons dried

2 tablespoons fresh dill or 2 teaspoons dried

4 tablespoons chopped fresh basil or 1 tablespoon dried

2 teaspoons salt

This recipe is reminiscent of one my mother used to make for family gatherings and picnics. I can still see the giant Tupperware container filled with colorful, crunchy vegetables. I loved it as a child. It was fresh, tangy, sweet, and crunchy all at once. Little did I know then how timeless this recipe would become.

Prepare the vegetables by chopping them into large bite-sized pieces (leave the cherry tomatoes whole). In a large saucepan, place the vegetables (except the cherry tomatoes and olives, if using) in a steamer basket set over water and cover the pan. Steam the vegetables for about 3 to 4 minutes—they should be brightly colored but still crunchy. Immediately remove from the heat and submerge the vegetables in cold or iced water. Drain, add the tomatoes and olives, if using, and set aside.

While the vegetables cool, whisk together the olive oil, vinegars, maple syrup, mustard, thyme, dill, basil, and salt. Pour the marinade over the cooled vegetables. Chill overnight if possible.

THE FAMILY KITCHEN

For kids who are old enough to chop, there is plenty of chopping to do. Younger kids can help break up the broccoli and cauliflower and cut zucchini or green beans with a butter knife. They can also help make the marinade and pour it over the veggies when ready. Best of all, they can watch it go into the giant Tupperware and keep an eye on it until picnic time.

Potato-Broccoli Salad ❦

SERVES 10 TO 12

8 medium red or yellow potatoes, cut into 1-inch pieces

4 tablespoons olive oil

1/4 cup cider vinegar

1 teaspoon salt

1/4 to 1/3 cup mayonnaise (use soy mayonnaise for vegan version)

2 tablespoons Dijon mustard

4 cloves garlic, minced

1 small red onion, chopped

1 1/2 to 2 pounds broccoli, peeled and chopped, including the top third of the stems

3 tablespoons chopped fresh dill (see Growing Green Flavor, page 64) or 1 tablespoon dried

It is hard not to love a good potato salad, but sometimes you are looking for something more than a pure carbohydrate fix. This salad is a classic-style potato salad, but with the added crunch of bright green, nutritious broccoli. At this time of year, with a great variety of potatoes available, we can have a dish that both satisfies the craving for comfort and provides a balance of nutrients.

Boil the potatoes until soft, cool them in ice water, and drain. Combine the potatoes with 2 tablespoons of the oil and the vinegar, salt, mayonnaise, and mustard.

Heat the other 2 tablespoons of oil and sauté the garlic and onions. After about 3 minutes, add the broccoli and 2 tablespoons of water and heat until the broccoli is bright green and softened, about 3 minutes. Let the mixture cool and then add it and the dill to the potatoes.

Gingered Green Beans ✦

SERVES 8 TO 10

1½ pounds green beans, stem ends removed

3 inches fresh ginger, peeled and minced

¼ cup toasted sesame oil

¼ cup orange juice

¼ cup champagne vinegar

2 teaspoons salt

One of the appealing aspects of this recipe is its simplicity. Given the limited number of ingredients, the result is surprisingly full of taste. The sweet and savory mix of the Asian flavors complements the crispness of fresh green beans.

Preheat the oven to 400 degrees. Combine the green beans with the ginger, sesame oil, orange juice, vinegar, and salt and toss to coat. Roast the beans for 15 to 20 minutes. Serve the beans right away for peak texture and flavor.

THE FAMILY KITCHEN

The kids can help remove the stem ends from the green beans—with or without knives. And if they nibble on a few raw beans while helping to prepare the recipe, all the better.

Quinoa and Cucumber Salad ❋

SERVES 10 TO 12

SALAD:

2 large cucumbers, halved and sliced

2 cups quinoa cooked in 4 cups water (see Cooking Grains, page 48)

1 sweet onion, sliced thinly

1/2 cup currants

1 bunch chard (or other greens like spinach, lacinato kale, or mustard), stemmed and finely chopped

1 cup toasted cashews or pecans (see Toasting Nuts, page 27)

DRESSING:

1/4 cup toasted sesame oil

1/4 cup safflower or canola oil

1/2 cup rice vinegar

2 tablespoons honey (use agave syrup for vegan version)

2 tablespoons prepared mustard

2 tablespoons tamari

1/4 cup orange or apple juice

1 teaspoon salt

I created this recipe because I really wanted a cool summery grain salad, but something other than tabbouleh (nothing against that wonderful dish, but there's more to life than mint). It is a joy to cook with sesame oil—its nutty flavor stands up to cooking and adds a wonderful layer of complexity to any dish. The fresh notes of honey and juice balance the tartness of the mustard, and the crisp cucumber and tangy currants are an unusual match finished by the sweet crunch of the nuts. The raw greens work fine in this salad as the small pieces soften in the dressing but maintain their integrity as well as their bright color.

Combine the salad ingredients in a large bowl. In a small bowl, whisk together the dressing ingredients until well mixed. Pour the dressing over the salad. Mix well and refrigerate until very cold. Serve as is or over a bed of greens.

THE FAMILY KITCHEN

In addition to chopping cucumbers and chard leaves, this recipe has a lot of room for variation, so encourage the kids to taste and describe the flavors, and come up with other ingredients to add or to use as substitutes for those listed.

Asian Pesto Rice Noodles with Mock Duck *

SERVES 6 TO 8

PESTO:

4 cups fresh basil leaves (see Growing Green Flavor, page 64)

6 cups fresh cilantro leaves

8 cloves garlic

2 jalapeños, stemmed and seeded

3/4 cup lemon juice

4 inches fresh ginger, peeled

3/4 cup toasted sesame oil

1 1/2 cups peanuts

3 tablespoons tamari

NOODLES AND MOCK DUCK:

1 pound rice noodles (fettuccini style or very thin will work well—I generally prefer the wider noodles for this recipe)

1 (14-ounce) can mock duck (seitan) or about 1 pound of the natural foods version (usually near the tofu in the market) or small pieces of beef or chicken

5 cups bite-sized pieces of mixed vegetables such as broccoli, onions, carrots, or peppers

2 tablespoons toasted sesame oil

1 tablespoon tamari

Pesto is simply a delicious and inspired combination of herbs, nuts, and spices. This is a wonderful and very different version that combines cilantro, basil, jalapeños, lemon, ginger, and sesame oil with peanuts. The result is a classic pesto texture with explosive and complementary flavors. This pesto is perfect for rice noodles and mock duck or any other hearty protein from tofu to beef.

To make the pesto, combine the basil, cilantro, garlic, jalapeños, lemon juice, ginger, sesame oil, peanuts, and tamari in a food processor. Pulse the food processor until all of the ingredients are finely chopped and blended into a smooth paste.

Meanwhile, bring 4 cups of water to a boil. Turn off the burner and add the rice noodles. Soak the noodles just until they soften, about 5 to 10 minutes, and then drain them and set them aside.

Prepare the mock duck by chopping it into pieces and browning it in a large skillet or wok (if you're using beef or chicken, cook thoroughly). Remove from the pan and then sauté the vegetables in the oil and tamari until the colors brighten, about 5 to 8 minutes. In a large serving dish, combine the noodles with the pesto and then fold in the mock duck and vegetables.

THE FAMILY KITCHEN

Cutting mock duck is a really fun activity and a good introduction to nonmeat proteins. Kids tend to enjoy the meatiness of it, without having to deal with the fat or chewiness of real meat. If you are looking for something gluten free, plain tofu and tempeh are great alternatives.

Fresh Potato and Smoked Salmon Salad

SERVES 8 TO 10

8 medium red or yellow potatoes, cut into 1-inch cubes

1 cup sun-dried tomatoes, softened in hot water, drained, and cut into pieces

4 tablespoons olive oil

1/4 cup cider vinegar

1 teaspoon salt

1/4 to 1/3 cup regular or soy mayonnaise

2 tablespoons Dijon mustard

4 cloves garlic, minced

2 medium leeks or 1 bunch spring onions, rinsed and minced

2 cups fresh spinach, chopped

1/4 cup chopped fresh basil (see Growing Green Flavor, page 64) or 2 tablespoons dried

12 ounces smoked salmon, broken into large pieces

This is a sassy variation on classic potato salad. The Midwest has some great sources for smoked salmon: Star Prairie Trout Farm sells smoked salmon as well as trout, and from Lake Superior's North Shore, Lou's Fish House and Russ Kendall's Smoke House are among some of the best. When you mix the mellow salmon with the fresh potatoes, you will know it is summer. This recipe encourages you to slow down and enjoy the flavors, so it is ideal for a Sunday brunch. The apple cider vinegar and Dijon mustard allow for a light hand with the mayonnaise, leaving you with loads of flavor but more healthful proportions.

Boil the potatoes until they're soft and drain them. Place the potatoes in a large bowl and add the sun-dried tomatoes, 2 tablespoons of the olive oil, vinegar, salt, mayonnaise, and mustard. Heat the other 2 tablespoons of oil and sauté the garlic and leeks. When these are soft (about 3 minutes), add the basil and spinach, wilt for about 30 seconds, and remove the pan from the heat. Add the sautéed vegetables to the potatoes and mix well. Stir in the salmon. Chill until ready to serve.

THE FAMILY KITCHEN

Smoked fish is not loved by all kids, but it is worth a try. If they do like it, allowing them to pull out the bones and crumble the fish into the mixture can be quite satisfying, and may expose them to another view of the fish they are about to eat. They can certainly help with the sun-dried tomatoes and the greens.

Potato Gratin with Gorgonzola

SERVES 10 TO 12

12 medium potatoes,
sliced in 1/4-inch rounds

1/2 cup olive oil, plus
2 tablespoons

2 teaspoons salt

1/4 cup balsamic vinegar

1 large red onion or leek,
sliced

4 cloves garlic, minced

2 zucchini, thinly sliced
(about 1 1/2 to 2 cups)

1/2 pound mushrooms, thinly
sliced (about 1 1/2 to 2 cups)

2 bell peppers, thinly sliced
(about 1 1/2 to 2 cups)

1 tablespoon minced fresh
thyme (see Growing Green
Flavor, page 64) or
1 teaspoon dried

1/4 cup chopped fresh basil or
1 tablespoon dried

2 cups quinoa cooked in
4 cups water (see Cooking
Grains, page 48)

2 fresh tomatoes, sliced thinly

2 tablespoons prepared
mustard

1 to 1 1/2 cups Gorgonzola
cheese

As children, most of us loved cheese and potatoes, especially when combined. This is the grown-up version of a much-loved comfort food. With the addition of quinoa and lots of vegetables, you can serve this as a healthful main course. Enjoy this with sautéed greens or a hearty salad.

Preheat the oven to 385 degrees. Coat the potatoes well with 1/4 cup of the olive oil and the salt, spread them evenly in a large, shallow baking pan, and bake, stirring often, until very tender, about 20 to 25 minutes.

Meanwhile, heat 2 tablespoons of the olive oil in a large skillet over medium heat, add the vinegar, and sauté the onion, garlic, zucchini, mushrooms, pepper, thyme, and basil until the vegetables are tender and brightly colored, about 5 minutes.

Spread the quinoa across the bottom of a deep baking pan and layer two-thirds of the potatoes on top of the quinoa. Place the sautéed vegetables on top of the potatoes and top with the remaining potatoes. Stir together the remaining 1/4 cup of olive oil and the mustard and drizzle it over the potatoes. Lay the tomatoes on top and sprinkle with the cheese. Bake until the cheese bubbles, about 15 minutes.

Southwestern Chicken Salad with Cilantro and Orange Dressing

SERVES 8 TO 10

SALAD:

2 pounds (4 to 5) boneless chicken breasts

2 cloves garlic, peeled and slice in half lengthwise

Olive oil

Salt

1 bunch green onions, minced

6 stalks celery, chopped

2 small red bell peppers, diced

1 cup frozen corn kernels, thawed

DRESSING:

1/2 cup olive oil

2 tablespoons toasted sesame oil

1/2 cup champagne vinegar

1/2 cup orange juice

1/2 cup tahini or mayonnaise

1 tablespoon stone-ground mustard

1/2 cup (about 1/2 bunch) chopped fresh cilantro (see Growing Green Flavor, page 64)

1 tablespoon chili powder

1 tablespoon cumin

1 teaspoon salt

Chicken salad is always popular, and the Mexican flavor palette in this recipe will ensure its status as a summer favorite. You'll achieve an unusual creaminess if you use tahini instead of mayonnaise. The lively spices reflect the salad's beautiful colors.

Preheat the oven to 350 degrees. Rub the chicken breasts with the cut side of the garlic, a dash of salt, and about a tablespoon of olive oil and place them in a roasting pan. Bake the chicken breasts for 20 to 25 minutes or until the juices run clear. Allow the chicken to cool, then slice or chop it into small pieces.

Meanwhile, make the dressing. In a small bowl, whisk together the oils, vinegar, orange juice, tahini, and mustard. Stir in the cilantro, chili powder, cumin, and salt.

Combine the cooked chicken with the onions, celery, peppers, and corn. Add some of the dressing and stir until well mixed. There may be more dressing than needed, so taste as you go, adding more dressing if needed. For a wonderful touch, top with a dollop of Montrachet or chèvre (look for Stickney Hill, Poplar Hill, or Donnay).

Harvest Lasagna ⓥ

SERVES 10 TO 12

LASAGNA SAUCE:

1 tablespoon olive oil

1 large onion, sliced

1 clove garlic, chopped

3 (14-ounce) cans diced tomatoes

1/8 cup sherry vinegar

1 tablespoon minced fresh oregano (see Growing Green Flavor, page 64) or 2 teaspoons dried

1 tablespoon chopped fresh basil or 2 teaspoons dried

1 teaspoon salt

1/2 cup tomato puree

FILLING:

1/4 cup olive oil

1 onion, sliced

4 cloves garlic, chopped

2 medium red kuri squash, peeled and seeded, quartered lengthwise, and sliced thinly

1 small eggplant, sliced

Eggplant, zucchini, peppers, onions, sautéed greens, and pesto ricotta turn this classic dish into a virtual feast of the season. Topped off with fresh, locally made mozzarella, just one piece of this lasagna is a filling, satisfying meal. The sauce is fragrant and flavorful and works for pizza too.

To make the sauce, heat the olive oil in a saucepan over medium heat and sauté the onions and garlic for 3 to 4 minutes. Add the diced tomatoes, vinegar, oregano, basil, and salt and simmer for 5 minutes. Then add the tomato puree and simmer another 10 minutes. This will make about 5 cups of sauce— plenty for the lasagna recipe, with a little left over to keep in the refrigerator (up to 1 week) or freezer.

> **THE FAMILY KITCHEN**
>
> Kids will enjoy mixing the pesto into the ricotta, and best of all, they will love to help put the whole thing together. Let them layer each item, from sauce to noodles to ricotta to vegetables.

To make the filling, heat the olive oil in a large saucepan and sauté the onion, garlic, and squash. Add 2/3 cup of water and let the squash steam in the covered pan for 10 to 15 minutes until it is soft. Move the squash mixture to a bowl and set it

(continued)

2 small zucchini, chopped into 1-inch pieces

1/2 head of broccoli, chopped into 1-inch pieces

1 red bell pepper, chopped into 1-inch pieces

3 cups spinach leaves, stemmed and coarsely chopped

2 teaspoons minced fresh thyme or 1 teaspoon dried thyme

2 teaspoons salt

1/2 cup Basil–Walnut pesto (page 23)

3 cups ricotta cheese (use tofu "cheese," recipe page 91, for vegan version)

1 package lasagna noodles, prepared according to package directions

1¹/2 cups fresh mozzarella, grated or crumbled (use tofu cheese for vegan version)

aside. Add the eggplant, zucchini, broccoli, and red pepper to the saucepan and sauté for 2 to 3 minutes, then add the spinach, thyme, and salt, and remove the pan from the heat. In a separate bowl, combine the pesto with the ricotta cheese.

Preheat the oven to 375 degrees. To assemble the lasagna, spread lasagna sauce to cover the bottom of a 9×13-inch pan. Cover the sauce with a layer of noodles, then layers of ricotta, squash, and vegetables. Add two more layers of sauce, noodles, ricotta, squash, and vegetables. Finish with a layer of noodles, then top the noodles with sauce and mozzarella cheese. Cover the pan with foil and bake for 40 minutes. Remove the foil and bake for another 15 minutes. The cheese should be browned and bubbly, and the noodles should be tender and moist.

Tofu "Cheese" ✤

1 pound extra-firm tofu

6 tablespoons nutritional yeast (the yellow flakey kind)

4 tablespoons balsamic vinegar

¼ cup nut butter of your choice (any type except peanut butter works)

1 teaspoon salt

This is a great cheese substitute that is full of flavor and is certain to please everyone, whether they are vegan or not! I use it for a number of the recipes throughout the book. It works great as an alternative to cheese or meat toppings for pizza or in lasagna—essentially any place you would normally use moist cheeses such as ricotta, feta, mozzarella, or chèvre. It browns nicely for baking in the oven, and has a tangy, smoky, and yeasty flavor.

Mash all of the ingredients together well with a fork—do not use a food processor or a blender. The mixture should be slightly lumpy, like the texture of crumbly cheese or browned ground meat. Store the "cheese" in the refrigerator for use as needed. It should last at least a week.

Curried Chickpeas and Autumn Vegetables ❦

SERVES 6 TO 8

2 tablespoons olive oil

2 tablespoons toasted sesame oil

2 leeks, rinsed and sliced

2 medium carrots, sliced

1 small eggplant, diced

1 red bell pepper, diced

1/2 head broccoli, peeled and chopped (including top half of stem)

1/2 head cauliflower, chopped

4 cloves garlic, minced

2 inches ginger, peeled and minced

1 tablespoon turmeric

1 tablespoon cumin

1 tablespoon chili powder

2 teaspoons minced fresh thyme (see Growing Green Flavor, page 64) or 1 teaspoon dried

2 teaspoons ground cayenne or dried red chili flakes

2 teaspoons salt

1 cup apple juice

1 (14-ounce) can coconut milk

2 cups chickpeas cooked in 6 cups water (see Cooking Beans and Legumes, page 7)

1/2 cup vegetable stock or water if needed (see Making Stock, page 38)

It is fun to infuse a familiar combination of fall vegetables with ethnic flavoring. Curries are a great way to create a delicious, fairly quick, and wholesome dish. My friend Raghavan Iyer, a chef and cookbook author, has educated me that curry is not the orange powder that comes already mixed together from the spice shop, but simply means a type of sauce—possibly creamy, spicy, or tomato based, depending on the region of origin. This curry is a turmeric-based sauce infused with coconut milk, sweet apple juice, and fresh garlic and ginger. Feel free to substitute other seasonal vegetables like green beans, turnips, and beets.

Heat the oils in a pan over medium heat, add the leeks and carrots, and sauté for about 3 minutes, until the leeks are soft. Add the eggplant, red pepper, broccoli, cauliflower, garlic, and ginger and sauté for another 5 minutes. Add the turmeric, cumin, chili powder, thyme, cayenne, salt, and apple juice and continue to cook on low heat for another 5 minutes, making sure the spices are well blended. Add the coconut milk and chickpeas and combine well. Turn the heat to low and let simmer for about 20 minutes. If the curry seems too thick, thin it with stock as needed. Serve over cooked grain.

Shepherd's Pie ⓥ

SERVES 10 TO 12

2 tablespoons olive oil

6 to 8 cups mixed diced vegetables such as onions, peppers, yams, carrots, broccoli, and greens

3 cloves garlic, minced

4 tablespoons minced fresh thyme (see Growing Green Flavor, page 64) or 2 teaspoons dried

1 cup milk (use rice milk for vegan version)

2 teaspoons salt

1 tablespoon celery seed

1 tablespoon cumin

6 to 8 pounds potatoes, diced

4 cups water

1/2 cup Basil–Walnut pesto (page 23)

1 pound ground meat (beef, bison, pork, or turkey), browned and crumbled (optional)

This is a favorite for adults and kids alike. Simply gather every vegetable that is in season, sauté them with a few herbs and spices, and top them with mashed potatoes for a comforting, satisfying, and nourishing meal. Some people like to add cheese or even meat to the topping. However you choose to combine them, the flavors taste like home and happiness.

Heat the oil in a large skillet over medium heat and sauté the mixed vegetables, garlic, and 2 tablespoons of the thyme. Add the milk and salt. When the vegetables are well cooked but not mushy, add the celery seed, cumin, and remaining 2 tablespoons of thyme. Set aside.

Boil the potatoes until they are very soft. Drain the potatoes and mash them with pesto. (If using meat, cook it in a separate skillet until it is browned and crumbly and combine with the vegetables now.)

Preheat the oven to 375 degrees. Divide the vegetables between two 9×13-inch baking pans and spread them evenly. Use a spatula to spread potatoes evenly over the top of the vegetables. Bake for 30 minutes.

> **THE FAMILY KITCHEN**
>
> My kids love mashed potatoes. This is a really fun way to use them and combine them with other vegetables, without mixing them together, which many kids don't really like. Kids can definitely help mash the potatoes. Whether you are going for the very creamy food processor version or the more rustic hand-mashed version, it is fun to mash and just as fun to spread the potatoes like frosting over the pie. As always, they can help to cut other vegetables as well.

Autumn Pasta with Tarragon and Cider Sauce ⓥ

SERVES 8 TO 10

2 medium butternut or red kuri squash, peeled and diced into 1-inch pieces

6 tablespoons olive oil, plus additional for serving

2 teaspoons salt

3 red bell peppers, roasted, peeled, and sliced (see Roasted Red Pepper and Leek Sauce on page 29 for roasting directions)

2 tablespoons walnut oil

2 leeks, rinsed and sliced into thin rings

6 cloves garlic, minced

1 cup walnuts, toasted and chopped (see Toasting Nuts, page 27)

1/2 cup fresh tarragon leaves (see Growing Green Flavor, page 64), chopped, or 2 tablespoons dried

1 cup fresh basil leaves, chopped, or 1/4 cup dried

1/4 cup sherry vinegar

1/2 cup apple cider

1/2 bunch lacinato kale, spinach, or chard, stemmed and torn into small pieces

1 pound fresh whole grain fettuccini or linguini

1/4 cup grated Asiago or Parmesan (omit for vegan version)

This recipe highlights the colors and flavors of autumn. Fresh tarragon adds a piney and aromatic taste that is mellowed by the sweetness of the cider. Quality whole grain pasta is hearty enough to handle the density of the squash, the depth of the roasted peppers, and the sweet caramel-like nature of the cider.

Preheat the oven to 400 degrees. Coat the squash with 4 tablespoons (1/4 cup) of the olive oil and the salt and roast for about 25 minutes, until the squash is very tender. Meanwhile, prepare the peppers and set them aside.

Heat the remaining 2 tablespoons of olive oil and the walnut oil in a large skillet over medium heat and sauté the leeks and garlic for about 3 minutes. When soft, add the red peppers, walnuts, tarragon, basil, vinegar, and squash and stir until well mixed. Add the apple cider and simmer for a minute, then add the greens and cover the pan. Cook for 30 seconds, just until the greens are wilted, then remove the pan from the heat immediately.

In a large pot, bring 6 cups of water to a rolling boil and cook the noodles until they are tender but not too soft, about 10 minutes. Drain the pasta in a colander and cool slightly under running water. Combine the vegetables with the cooked pasta, toss with some additional olive oil, and sprinkle with grated Asiago or Parmesan cheese.

Polenta with Chicken and Artichoke-Tomato Sauce

MAKES 10 TO 12 SERVINGS

3 cups water

1 cup polenta

7 tablespoons olive oil

2 onions, sliced thin

6 cloves garlic, minced

2 red bell peppers, diced

2 cups mushrooms, sliced

2 tablespoons chopped fresh basil (see Growing Green Flavor, page 64) or 2 teaspoons dried

1 tablespoon chopped fresh rosemary or 1 teaspoon dried

1 teaspoon salt

4 cups diced fresh tomatoes or 2 (14-ounce) cans diced tomatoes

2 cups canned and drained artichoke hearts

1 cup red wine

2 tablespoons miso paste

2 tablespoons maple syrup

1/4 cup unbleached flour

1 cup water

Polenta is most often thought of as comfort food. In this dish, it is presented with the rich, elegant flavor of garlic and artichokes. It is easy to prepare, so it's a perfect choice for a dinner with friends when you want them to feel special, yet you want to have time to enjoy their company.

Bring the water to a boil, then slowly add the polenta, whisking regularly to remove lumps. Simmer the mixture and continue stirring it for about 5 minutes. Remove the polenta from the heat and spread it in a 9×13-inch pan to cool.

In a large skillet, heat 2 tablespoons of olive oil over medium heat and sauté the onion, garlic, peppers, and mushrooms. Add the basil, rosemary, salt, tomatoes, artichokes, red wine, miso, and maple syrup. In a small bowl whisk the flour and water together until creamy and stir into the tomato mixture to thicken it.

In a separate pan, heat 1 tablespoon of olive oil over medium heat and brown the chicken or tofu until it's cooked through. Add the chicken or tofu to the sauce and simmer over low heat for about 15 minutes.

THE FAMILY KITCHEN

The kids can use cookie cutters to help make different shapes with the cooled polenta. Also, have them whisk the flour and water together and stir it into the mixture to see how it thickens the sauce. This is kitchen chemistry at work.

(continued)

2 pounds chicken or tofu, cut into large pieces about 1 inch by 2 inches

1/2 to 1 cup thinly shaved or grated Asiago or other flavorful cheese (optional)

Cut the polenta into shapes—triangles, circles, or squares— about 2 inches across. In a large skillet, heat the remaining 4 tablespoons of olive oil and brown the polenta on all sides. Serve with a generous spoonful of sauce on top. If you like, sprinkle grated or thinly shaved Asiago or another flavorful cheese on top.

Pumpkin Ravioli with Corn Cream Sauce

PASTA DOUGH:

1½ cups semolina flour, finest grind

1½ cups flour (I usually use about half whole wheat flour, but whole wheat will result in a drier dough, so you might need to add some moisture)

1 teaspoon salt

4 eggs

2 tablespoons extra-virgin olive oil

FILLING:

2 tablespoons butter or olive oil

1 onion, minced

2 pounds (about 2 medium) pumpkin, peeled and cubed

6 cloves garlic, minced

¼ cup minced fresh herbs such as sage, thyme, rosemary (see Growing Green Flavor, page 64)

1 teaspoon nutmeg

2 teaspoon salt

½ cup water

1 cup buttermilk or yogurt

This is an elegant dish so full of flavor that it will likely be requested frequently by family and friends. For the sauce, I use Hope Creamery butter. It's my favorite for so many reasons. The creamery is a family-run business. Their butter is made from the thickest cream from grass-fed cows raised on small local dairy farms. And they churn in small batches that are never frozen. Since I'm mentioning favorites, Cedar Summit Farm is another of my favorite sources for exceptional dairy products. Not only is their unhomogenized milk thick and golden with a half inch of pure cream on the top of every jar, but the cream jar itself is adorable and worth saving to use as a vase for flowers.

To make the pasta dough, place the flours in a food processor fitted with a metal blade. Add the salt, eggs, and olive oil. Process until the dough begins to mass on the blade (about 1 to 2 minutes). Remove the dough from the processor and press it into a ball. Wrap the dough in plastic and let it rest at least 2 hours in the refrigerator before rolling and cutting it.

THE FAMILY KITCHEN

This recipe is perfect for getting everyone involved in cooking. Kids can collaborate on everything from making the pasta dough to mashing the pumpkin to assembling the pillows of completely delicious flavors. This is a recipe where you can allow for variations in the shape and size of the ravioli.

Note: The pasta dough can also be made by hand or in an electric mixer fitted with a dough hook. For each of these

(continued)

CORN CREAM SAUCE:

1/4 cup butter

2 shallots, minced

2 cloves garlic, minced

2 cups corn kernels, cut off the cob, or frozen

1 teaspoon salt

1 teaspoon pepper

2 teaspoons chopped fresh thyme or 1 teaspoon dried

1 1/2 cups fresh cream

methods, mix the dry ingredients together first, make a well in the center, add the wet ingredients, and mix them together slowly until everything is combined well.

Meanwhile, make the filling. Heat the butter in a large skillet over medium heat and sauté the onion. Add the pumpkin, garlic, herbs, nutmeg, salt, and water. Cover and allow the pumpkin to cook until soft, about 10 minutes. Add the buttermilk and blend well, cover, and heat for another 3 to 5 minutes. Remove from the heat and let cool at least until it is not too hot to touch. Mash it all together really well either in a food processor or by hand (a fork or sturdy wire whisk will work for this).

Roll out the chilled pasta dough on a floured surface to no more than 1/4-inch thick and cut it into uniform 2-inch squares (there are special tools for cutting ravioli, and circles are fine too). Place a small spoonful of filling into the center of a square of dough, top it with another square of dough, and seal the edges well with a fork. Bring a stockpot of water to a rolling bowl, drop in the ravioli pillows, and cook them for about 5 minutes.

To make the sauce, heat the butter in a saucepan, add the shallots and garlic, and sauté for 2 minutes. Add the corn, salt, pepper, and thyme, and then slowly pour in the cream. Continue to heat over low heat until the cream thickens. Remove the pan from the heat and spoon the sauce over the cooked ravioli.

Mediterranean Succotash with Edamame and Lime ⓥ

SERVES 10 TO 12

2 tablespoons olive oil

2 tablespoons toasted
sesame oil

2 leeks, rinsed and sliced

6 cloves garlic, minced

2 red bell peppers, diced

1 cup dried navy or cannellini
beans cooked in 2½ cups
water (see Cooking Beans
and Legumes, page 7)

2 teaspoons salt

Juice of 1 lime

½ cup water

2 tablespoons cumin

3 cups fresh or frozen shelled
edamame (green soy beans),
cooked

1 cup fresh basil leaves
(see Growing Green Flavor,
page 64), minced

1 cup (about ½ pound) feta,
crumbled (use tofu for vegan
version)

2 eggs, whipped (omit for
vegan version)

1 cup fine bread crumbs
(panko, a prepared bread
crumb product available in
most grocery stores, is a great
alternative to making your
own bread crumbs)

*This works perfectly as a main dish, but can also work as a side
dish with fish, chicken, or tofu. The recipe can also be prepared
completely vegan by substituting a cup of crumbled tofu for the
eggs and cheese.*

Heat the oils, sauté the leeks for 2 to 3 minutes, then add
the garlic, red peppers, and beans and continue to sauté for
another 4 to 5 minutes. Add the salt, lime juice, water, cumin,
and edamame. Bring the bean mixture to a simmer over
medium heat and then add the basil, cheese, eggs, and bread
crumbs. Heat through.

African Peanut Stew with Spiced Millet ✴

SERVES 8 TO 10

3 large yams, peeled and diced

1¹/₂ cups garbanzo beans cooked in 4 to 5 cups water (see Cooking Beans and Legumes, page 7) or 1 (25-ounce) can

3 red bell peppers, diced

¹/₄ cup olive oil

2 medium onions, diced

8 cloves garlic, minced

2 tablespoons cumin

1 tablespoon coriander

2 cups peanut butter (I prefer natural crunchy peanut butter for this dish)

6 tablespoons tamari

²/₃ cup lemon juice

3 cups water or vegetable stock (see Making Stock, page 38)

This truly is peanut butter soup. It has a nice thick texture and works with lots of different greens and vegetables. If you are not a fan of the peanut, you can still savor this stew by substituting other nut butters. It is a lovely warm and hearty stew that combines very nicely with the millet.

In a stockpot, steam the yams for 10 minutes in a half-inch of water and then add the beans. In a skillet, sauté the red peppers in olive oil for 2 to 3 minutes, then add the onions, garlic, cumin, and coriander. Sauté for another minute and then transfer the contents of the skillet to a food processor and add the peanut butter, tamari, lemon juice, and 2 cups of the water or stock. Process until well blended. Pour this peanut sauce over the beans and veggies and add another ¹/₂ to 1 cup of the water or stock as needed. Heat through.

THE FAMILY KITCHEN

It is hard for kids not to take interest in the fact that you are making soup with peanut butter. They may be skeptical at first, but bring them into the process and perhaps they will give it a taste. It is actually very satisfying and tasty.

SPICED MILLET:

2 tablespoons olive oil

1 tablespoon cumin

1 teaspoon cayenne pepper

1 teaspoon cinnamon

1½ cups diced red bell pepper

2½ cups millet

5 cups water

1 cup (about 1 bunch) minced fresh cilantro

1 teaspoon salt

Prepare the spiced millet while the stew heats. Heat the olive oil in a large saucepan over medium heat and sauté the cumin, cayenne, cinnamon, and red pepper. Add the millet, water, and cilantro. Cover and bring to a boil, then turn down the heat and simmer for about 15 minutes, until the water is absorbed and the grain is fluffy. Serve the stew over the millet.

Lentil-Walnut Burgers ⓥ

SERVES 8

1/4 cup corn oil

1 medium onion, diced

2 carrots, diced

5 stalks celery, diced

3 cloves garlic, minced

1 tablespoon dried dill

1 tablespoon dried thyme

2 tablespoons prepared
mustard

1/2 cup mayonnaise
(use soy mayonnaise for
vegan version)

1 cup walnuts, chopped finely
(this can be done in a food
processor)

1 cup small capers, rinsed
and drained

2 cups brown lentils cooked
in 4 cups water (see Cooking
Beans and Legumes, page 7)

1 to 2 cups brown rice flour

These meatless burgers are full of rich and savory flavor. The recipe provides a good basic formula, and you can experiment with different legumes and nuts for flavor and texture.

Heat the oil in a skillet and sauté the onion, carrots, celery, and garlic until very soft. Add the dill, thyme, mustard, mayonnaise, nuts, and capers. Combine this mixture with the cooked lentils in a bowl. Transfer half of the mixture to a food processor and puree it. Return the pureed mixture to the bowl, add about a cup of the brown rice flour, and stir to combine. The mixture should be firm but not crumbly. If it seems flimsy and too soft, add a little more rice flour. Form the mixture into patties and fry them in a frying pan until browned and heated through. Serve with your favorite "burger" condiments.

THE FAMILY KITCHEN

It probably goes without saying that many kids love this dish. There is a lot of handwork involved, which makes it an ideal recipe to make with younger children and can even be a lot of fun for teens wanting to enjoy vegetarian choices in their diets. Make sure they understand these are not your typical burgers; in fact, it may be wise to name them something else entirely.

Roasted-Squash Gratin with Cilantro Pesto

SERVES 8

1 large or 2 small butternut or other meaty squash, like kabocha or buttercup, peeled and cut into slices 1/2 inch thick and 2 inches wide (cut butternut squash in half lengthwise, then slice; cut round squash in quarters lengthwise and then slice)

3 carrots, cut thinly into long diagonal slices

3 medium gold beets, peeled and sliced

3 medium parsnips or turnips or a combination, peeled and sliced

1 red onion, sliced

1/4 cup olive oil

2 tablespoons balsamic vinegar

1/2 teaspoon salt

1/2 cup feta or blue cheese, crumbled (omit for vegan version)

1/2 cup grated Asiago or other hard cheese (omit for vegan version)

Chopped, pitted olives (optional)

Chopped or sliced tomatoes (optional)

This dish has a wonderful fragrance and is a visual treat as well. It is also a dish you can prepare the night before and then bake when needed. The layers of squash hide all kinds of little surprise flavors inside. Each bite is a burst of something yummy and different.

Preheat the oven to 350 degrees. Coat the squash, carrots, beets, parsnips, and onions with the olive oil, vinegar, and salt and roast, stirring regularly, until tender, about 15 to 20 minutes. Let the roasted vegetables cool enough to handle comfortably.

Prepare the cilantro pesto by combining the olive oil, garlic, cilantro, nuts, and salt in a food processor and processing to a smooth paste. Add more oil or cilantro as need to reach the texture you prefer.

THE FAMILY KITCHEN

This dish involves a lot of cutting, and kids will enjoy carefully turning the root vegetables into the slices that become the layers of this delicious gratin. Also, layering the different ingredients is a fun activity. You don't need to be too rigid about what goes where. Eventually it all ends up in your belly!

(continued)

CILANTRO PESTO:

¹/₄ cup olive oil

4 cloves garlic

1 bunch cilantro

¹/₂ cup toasted almonds or pecans

2 teaspoons salt

Turn the oven temperature up to 400 degrees. When the vegetables have cooled, layer the ingredients in a deep baking dish as follows: vegetables, pesto, feta, olives and tomatoes (if using). Repeat the layers and top with the Asiago. If you're preparing this to cook later, cover and refrigerate the dish now. Otherwise, bake for about 15 minutes, until the vegetables are heated through and the cheese is melted.

Black-Eyed Pea and Sweet Potato Ragout ✴

SERVES 8 TO 12

2 tablespoons olive oil

1 leek, rinsed and sliced

4 cloves garlic, minced

1 medium squash (butternut
works well) or 2 yams
(I prefer garnet), peeled and
diced into 1-inch cubes

$^{1}/_{2}$ cup water

5 stalks celery, diced

1 cup sun-dried tomatoes,
softened in hot water, drained,
and cut in $^{1}/_{4}$-inch pieces

2 tomatoes, diced (omit if
flavorful fresh tomatoes are
not available)

1$^{1}/_{2}$ cups dried black-eyed
peas cooked in 4 cups water
(see Cooking Beans and
Legumes, page 7)

DRESSING:

$^{1}/_{3}$ cup olive oil

$^{1}/_{4}$ cup raspberry vinegar

$^{1}/_{2}$ cup orange juice

2 tablespoons Dijon mustard

$^{1}/_{4}$ cup miso paste or
2 tablespoons Jack Daniels
whiskey

2 tablespoons minced fresh
thyme or 2 teaspoons dried

2 tablespoons cumin

2 teaspoons salt

*This dish has an attractive range of colors, and the black-eyed
peas contribute an unusual appearance and taste. They are not
commonly used, so this is a fun way to bring them back into the
cycle. The orange juice is tangy, the raspberry vinegar is sweet,
and the whiskey or miso adds an unusual bite to the dressing.
These flavors pull together the starchy black-eyed peas with the
creamy sweet potatoes.*

Heat the olive oil in a large skillet and sauté the leek, garlic,
and squash. Add the water, cover, and steam until the squash
is soft. Add the celery and sun-dried tomatoes to the pan and
sauté. Remove the pan from the heat and add the diced fresh
tomatoes. Drain any excess water. Combine the vegetables and
the black-eyed peas in a large bowl.

Whisk together all of the dressing ingredients. Pour the
dressing over the vegetables and black-eyed peas and stir to coat.

Stuffed Squash with Wild Rice, Quinoa, and Pine Nut Pilaf ⓥ

||||||||||||||||||||||||||||||||||||||||||||||||||||||||||||||||||||||||||||||||||||||||||||||||||||||||||||||||||||||||||||||||||||||||||||||

SERVES 6 TO 8

1 cup wild rice

1 cup barley

6 delicata or 2 acorn or
2 butternut squash

2 tablespoons olive oil

2 leeks, rinsed and chopped

4 cloves garlic, minced

1 red bell pepper, diced

1 tablespoon dried fenugreek

2 tablespoons cumin

1 tablespoon celery seed

1/2 cup champagne vinegar

2 teaspoons salt

2 dozen shiitake or other
mushrooms, sliced

2 cups toasted pine nuts
(see Toasting Nuts, page 27)

2 cups olives, pitted and
chopped

1 cup queso fresco or
Chihuahua cheese (use Tofu
Cheese, page 91, for vegan
version)

There are so many possible combinations for stuffing it is hard to choose. I love this one because it uses unusual grains, the pine nuts add a lovely sophistication, and the fenugreek has a special sweet caramel flavor that is hard to pinpoint but has a dramatic effect. Also, there are lots of ways to embellish this recipe—try olives or sun-dried tomatoes or additional veggies. Essentially, anything goes, and the more the better. I like to top this with a nice local Asiago or queso fresco–style sheep's milk cheese like Shepherd's Way Farms queso fresco. Steven Read and Jodi Ohlsen Read have been raising sheep and making extraordinary, award-winning cheeses since right around the time we started the Good Life Café. I used to get a full wheel of their now very hard to find Friesago, which is perhaps still my favorite cheese of all time. They have suffered some huge setbacks but have continued to persevere in their commitment to sustainable farming, creative approaches to small farm business, and world-class cheese production.

Combine the wild rice and the barley in a pot with 4 cups of water. Bring to a boil, reduce to a simmer, cover, and cook until tender, about 30 minutes. Set the cooked grains aside.

Preheat the oven to 350 degrees. Cut delicata squash in half and larger squash in thirds. Remove the seeds and bake the squash in a shallow baking dish until they are tender to a fork but not mushy, about 15 to 20 minutes. Set the squash aside.

In a large skillet, heat the olive oil over medium heat and sauté the leeks, garlic, red pepper, and fenugreek. Add the cumin, celery seed, vinegar, salt, and mushrooms and cook until the mushrooms are tender and moist, about 5 minutes. Combine the contents of the skillet with the grains and add the pine nuts and olives.

Raise the oven temperature to 375 degrees. Place a large scoop of stuffing into each portion of squash, top it with cheese, and heat in the oven until the cheese is brown and the squash is soft, about 10 minutes.

Squash–Pecan Croquettes

MAKES 12 TO 16
CROQUETTES

2 butternut squash, peeled
and cut into roughly 1-inch
cubes

2¹/₂ cups pecans

2 tablespoons toasted
sesame oil

1 cup millet, cooked in 2 cups
water (see Cooking Grains,
page 48)

2 teaspoons salt

2 tablespoons fresh thyme

1 tablespoon garlic powder

¹/₂ cup flour, if needed

2 tablespoons vegetable oil
for frying (optional)

This is a fun way to prepare whole grains. The recipe uses millet, though a similar croquette could be made with almost any grain (barley and short-grain brown rice work particularly well as they are sticky and round). The squash offers a rich and smooth base, and the pecans bring sweetness and also help to bind the croquettes. Herbs and spices round out the flavors. Croquettes can be fried like burgers or baked in smaller sizes, and they are wonderful with Ginger–Sesame Sauce (page 32).

Steam the squash in a shallow saucepan until it is very soft. Drain the water and mash the squash until it's smooth. Put the pecans and the toasted sesame oil in a blender and blend until the pecans are finely ground. Combine the squash with the cooked millet and ground pecans and add the salt, thyme, and garlic powder. The mixture should be soft but not runny. Add the flour only as needed to help the mixture hold together better. Form into rounds about the size of golf balls or into burger patties.

Croquettes can be fried in a skillet over medium heat until brown on both sides, or baked on an oiled pan for 20 to 25 minutes at 375 degrees, turning once until browned on both sides.

THE FAMILY KITCHEN

Making croquettes is a lot like making Lentil–Walnut Burgers (page 102). The kids enjoy forming the patties and balls.

Greek Squash or Pumpkin in Phyllo Casserole

SERVES 6 TO 8

2 large squash (butternut or kabocha is nice) or 1 medium pumpkin, cut in half and seeded

2 leeks, rinsed and sliced into rings

6 cloves garlic, minced

4 tablespoons olive oil

4 eggs, beaten

1 pound feta cheese, crumbled

1 tablespoon salt

1 tablespoon pepper

¼ cup maple syrup

1 package phyllo dough

This is a very unusual and delicious way to use squash. The squash or pumpkin meat is sautéed with leeks and garlic until creamy and tender, then combined with feta cheese and layered with phyllo. It is at once traditional and very modern. This dish is hearty on a cold evening, and filled with color and flavor. Phyllo dough is delicate and can be very tricky to handle. It's best to buy it frozen and allow it to thaw slowly. Unroll it gently and have a moist cloth (not a towel) handy. Keep the sheets flat and covered with the moist cloth while you're assembling this dish. Remove just one to two sheets at a time. If the phyllo gets gooey, your cloth is too wet.

Preheat the oven to 375 degrees. Place the squash facedown in a deep baking pan filled with a half inch of water. Bake until the squash is very soft. Remove the squash from the oven and let it cool. Then scrape the squash meat into a bowl and mash it.

In a large skillet, sauté the leeks and garlic in 2 tablespoons of the olive oil until soft, about 3 minutes. Add the leeks and garlic to the mashed squash along with the eggs and feta cheese. Season with salt and pepper, add the maple syrup, and combine evenly.

THE FAMILY KITCHEN

Although the phyllo needs to be handled with care, it is a fun ingredient to use. The kids can unroll the large sheets, and have a try at putting a layer or two of this dish together. They certainly can be ready with the oil to brush on top of the layers of dough. If you need to cut the dough, a pizza cutter can be an effective way to get a fairly straight line. Let the kids make an individual pie just to get a feel for working with the phyllo.

Grease a 7×11×2-inch baking pan. Fit one or two sheets of phyllo in the bottom of the pan, brush them with olive oil, then add another sheet or two of phyllo. Cover the phyllo with half the squash mixture. Place one or two sheets of phyllo on top of the squash, brush the top sheet with olive oil, and layer on yet another sheet or two of phyllo. Spread the rest of the squash mixture over the phyllo and top it with two final sheets of phyllo. Poke several holes through the top layer of phyllo (I find that a small paring knife works well for this) and brush it with olive oil. Bake for 35 to 40 minutes, or until the casserole is firm and nicely browned.

Turkey and Sheep-Cheese Quiche

**MAKES TWO 8- OR
9-INCH QUICHES**

CRUST:

¹/₃ **cup whole wheat pastry
flour**

¹/₃ **cup unbleached flour**

¹/₂ **cup cornmeal**

¹/₄ **cup butter (or olive oil)**

¹/₂ **to 1 cup ice water**

FILLING:

**1 small turkey breast (1 to
1¹/₂ pounds), chopped into
small pieces**

6 tablespoons olive oil

¹/₄ **cup plain yogurt**

**1 large or 2 small leeks,
rinsed and sliced**

6 cloves garlic, minced

**1 large head broccoli,
chopped (2 cups)**

**2 red bell peppers, roasted,
peeled, and chopped (see
Polenta with Tomato
Jam, page 3, for roasting
directions)**

*This is a wonderful way to use any leftover turkey from a
traditional Thanksgiving feast—or any other meal where you've
roasted a turkey. It is a light dish made flavorful with the roasted
peppers. The red and green of the peppers and broccoli add
festive color to the winter season.*

To make the crust, combine the flours and cornmeal in a bowl.
Cut in the butter or oil until evenly incorporated, and then mix
in the ice water. A note about making perfect dough in this
recipe: It should feel like an earlobe and be soft and moist, but
not sticky. You can work it with your hands until it feels very
smooth, kneading it lightly for just a minute until it is tender
and pliable. Divide the dough into two balls.

THE FAMILY KITCHEN

You can double the crust recipe to have a portion of
dough just for the kids to play with and shape, or to
make their own individual quiches—something my kids
love to do. Keep in mind that quiches need not be round;
any small pan of any shape will work. They can create
whatever combination of ingredients they want, and
design it however they like, which makes it even more
likely that they will eat it! Kids can also help roll the crust
out for the pie or quiche pan. It is not hard to find kid-
sized rolling pins at children's toy stores or even at some
kitchen stores. Small rolling pins and French rolling pins
are perfect for smaller hands and offer more control and
less mess. Kids will also enjoy fluting the edge of the
crusts, so long as they don't expect perfection.

1 pound (about 2 cups)
queso fresco or other similar
soft and fresh cheese, minced
or crumbled

6 large or extra-large eggs

1/2 cup cream

Salt and pepper

1 tablespoon minced fresh
thyme (see Growing Green
Flavor, page 64) or
2 teaspoons dried

Grease two quiche or pie pans. Roll out one ball of dough at a time on a floured surface or between two sheets of waxed paper. Roll from the center out in all directions—as if you were rolling out petals on a daisy—until you have a circle of dough about 2 inches larger than your pan and no more than 1/4 inch thick. Carefully fold the dough into a semicircle (if you used waxed paper, remove one sheet and fold the dough so the paper is inside), align it evenly over half of the pan, and unfold the dough to cover the entire pan with the dough hanging evenly over the edges. Gently press the dough into the pan (remove the other sheet of waxed paper). Work the overhanging dough into a fluted edge by wrapping it around a finger and pinching it every 2 inches or so.

Preheat the oven to 350 degrees. In a skillet, brown the diced turkey in 2 tablespoons of the olive oil and the yogurt until cooked, about 10 minutes. (If the turkey is already cooked, simply mix the cubed pieces with the oil and yogurt.) Move the turkey to a bowl. Heat the remaining olive oil and sauté the leeks until soft, then add the garlic and broccoli and sauté until the broccoli is bright green. Combine the broccoli with the peppers and turkey and spread it in the prepared crusts. Spread the cheese evenly over the filling. Whisk the eggs in a bowl until they're fluffy, then add the cream, salt, pepper, and thyme and pour over the vegetables. Bake for 25 minutes.

Winter Squash and Greens in Coconut Milk Curry *

SERVES 8 TO 10

2 medium squash such as butternut, red kuri, or pumpkin, peeled and cut
into 1-inch cubes

2 tablespoons olive oil

2 tablespoons toasted sesame oil

2 large leeks, rinsed and sliced

6 cloves garlic, minced

2 inches ginger, peeled and minced

1 tablespoon cumin

1 tablespoon coriander

1 tablespoon turmeric

1 tablespoon chili powder

2 teaspoons cinnamon

2 tablespoons minced fresh thyme (see Growing Green Flavor, page 64) or 2 teaspoons dried

1/4 cup lemon juice

1/4 cup sugar or maple syrup

2 large heads broccoli, cut into bite-sized pieces (about 6 cups)

2 teaspoons salt

1 (16-ounce) can coconut milk

1 cup toasted cashews (see Toasting Nuts, page 27) (optional)

1 pound mock duck or chicken breast, chopped and stir-fried until browned (optional)

2 cups brown rice cooked in 5 cups water (see Cooking Grains, page 48)

Not only is this winter curry beautiful, it is incredibly nutritious and delicious and a creative way to use squash and pumpkin. Winter squash, including pumpkin, perfectly complements any seasonal green. You can use broccoli, greens, or green beans depending upon the season. The coconut milk is creamy and rich, but not overly so.

Steam the squash in a large covered skillet until it is tender but not mushy, about 6 minutes. Remove any extra water from the pan and place the squash in a bowl.

In the same skillet, heat the oils. Add the leeks, garlic, ginger, and squash, and sauté until the leeks are soft. Add the cumin, coriander, turmeric, chili powder, cinnamon, thyme, lemon juice, and maple syrup. Mix well until the pumpkin is coated, then add the broccoli, salt, and coconut milk. Cover and allow to simmer until the broccoli is bright green, about 3 minutes. Then uncover, stir to make sure all of the vegetables are coated in the curry, add the cashews and mock duck if desired, and continue cooking until the squash is tender, about another 3 minutes. Serve immediately over brown rice.

Roasted Winter Vegetable Gratin ⓥ

SERVES 6 TO 8

3 medium potatoes, sliced in rounds

3 medium beets, peeled and sliced in rounds

1 butternut squash, peeled and cut into 1-inch cubes

6 tablespoons olive oil

1/4 cup balsamic vinegar

2 teaspoons salt

1 large red onion or leek, sliced

4 cloves garlic, minced

1 tablespoon minced fresh thyme (see Growing Green Flavor, page 64) or 1 teaspoon dried

1/4 cup chopped fresh basil or 2 tablespoons dried

4 to 6 cups chopped assorted vegetables (broccoli, cauliflower, zucchini, and peppers)

1 cup barley and 1 cup brown rice cooked together in 5 cups water (see Cooking Grains, page 48)

2 tomatoes, sliced thinly (omit the tomatoes if they are not in season)

1 cup of your favorite cheese—I enjoy a smooth and easily melted cheese like gruyere or a creamy chèvre (omit for vegan version)

Cooks in the Midwest have long embraced the notion of a casserole, and I think it's a wonderful characteristic. I am a big fan of getting as many delicious and wholesome ingredients into one pan as I can. Ask my husband and he will tell you, I am the queen of the one-pot meal, and proud of it! This is yet more proof that if you are thoughtful enough to combine similar flavors, and balance them with a few standouts, the results can be highly satisfying and well-rounded. This dish travels to holiday gatherings quite well too.

Preheat the oven to 385 degrees. Combine the potatoes, beets, and squash with 4 tablespoons (1/4 cup) of the olive oil, the balsamic vinegar, and salt. Make sure the vegetables are well coated and spread across the bottom of a deep baking pan. Roast, stirring frequently, until the vegetables are very tender, about 20 to 25 minutes.

Meanwhile, in the remaining 2 tablespoons of olive oil, sauté the onion, garlic, thyme, basil, and assorted chopped vegetables until the vegetables are tender and brightly colored, about 5 to 7 minutes.

Reduce the oven temperature to 350 degrees. Mix the barley and rice with the potatoes, beets, and squash until well combined and spread the mixture across the bottom of a 9×13-inch casserole dish. Layer the sautéed vegetables over top and then cover it all with the sliced tomatoes. Crumble or grate the cheese on top and bake until the cheese is browned and melted, about 10 minutes.

Pizza with Arugula, Potatoes, Caramelized Spring Onions, and Gouda or Gorgonzola

MAKES 2 LARGE (12-INCH) OR 6 SMALL (5-INCH) PIZZAS

CRUST:

2¹/₂ cups warm water

2 tablespoons dry yeast

¹/₈ cup honey

2 teaspoons salt

1 tablespoon dried basil

5 to 6 cups unbleached or whole wheat bread flour

TOPPING:

4 tablespoons olive oil

12 to 15 spring onions, rinsed and sliced into 1-inch pieces

¹/₄ cup balsamic vinegar

2 tablespoons maple syrup

1 cup fresh arugula, chopped

4 medium Yukon Gold potatoes, sliced paper thin

¹/₄ cup fresh rosemary, minced or 2 tablespoons dried

1 teaspoon salt

1 pound Gorgonzola or smoked Gouda, chilled

There is good reason pizza is so popular. The variations are endless. The toppings can be taken to a fine art form. But it always comes down to a good crust and a sauce that sings with flavor. This is that recipe. The crust can be used immediately or frozen to use later.

To make the dough, place the water in a bowl and add the yeast, honey, and salt. Let mixture begin to bubble (approximately 5 to 8 minutes), then add the basil. Add the flour one cup at a time and mix until doughy. The dough should be firm and pliable and not sticky. Knead the dough for about 5 minutes, then place it in a lightly oiled bowl. Cover the bowl with a moist towel and set it in warm place for the dough to rise. After approximately 40 minutes, punch down the dough and let it rise again.

THE FAMILY KITCHEN

Even the most persnickety eater in a family will be delighted on pizza night. Let the kids take control of what they choose to put on top of their pizza. In addition, don't be afraid to work with yeast. The few extra steps are worth the tasty outcome. If you follow the instructions and trust your senses and intuition, the dough will turn out well, and since you don't have to get a full rise for pizza crust, there truly is no reason to be intimidated. Even more, making pizza crust is an opportunity for your kids to observe yeast at work. You can talk about how the once-dry yeast comes "alive" in the warm water to transform the ingredients into a bubbling, living concoction. And as you work with the dough, everyone will gain an appreciation of the kneading process without expecting an artisan loaf. Soon enough, you will be rolling them out like a pro!

Preheat the oven to 375 degrees. After the second rising, cut the dough into pieces about the size of a tangerine for individual pizzas or triple that size for large pizzas. Use a rolling pin to roll out the dough on a floured surface. Prick the crusts with a fork or a knife, place them on a cookie sheet, and pre-bake them for 5 to 6 minutes.

Prepare the toppings while the dough is rising. Heat 2 tablespoons of the olive oil and add the onions. Stir to coat onions thoroughly, add the vinegar and maple syrup, bring to a boil over medium heat, then quickly lower the heat to a simmer and cover the pan. Stir occasionally and continue to cook for about 20 minutes. Then add the arugula and continue cooking for 5 minutes, until the onions are nicely browned.

Preheat the oven to 400 degrees. While the onions are cooking, coat the potatoes with the remaining 2 tablespoons of olive oil, the rosemary, and the salt. Spread the potatoes in a shallow baking pan and roast them, stirring often. The potatoes should be cooked through in about 10 minutes.

To assemble a pizza, layer potatoes over the crust and top the potatoes with caramelized onions. Sprinkle with nice chunks of gorgonzola or smoked Gouda and bake for about 6 minutes, until the cheese is bubbly and hot.

Barley "Risotto" with Wild Mushrooms, Leeks, and Sun-Dried Tomatoes ⓥ

SERVES 8 TO 10

1 cup barley

5 cups stock or water

1/2 cup olive oil

2 cloves garlic, minced

2 cups milk of your choice (use rice or soy milk for vegan version)

1/2 cup white wine

2 large leeks, rinsed and coarsely chopped (substitute two bunches of ramps if they are in season)

1 cup sun-dried tomatoes, soaked in 2 cups hot water and chopped or cut with scissors

1 cup sliced shiitake or cremini mushrooms

1 cup chopped fresh bacon or smoked turkey (omit for vegan version)

2 tablespoons minced fresh thyme (see Growing Green Flavor, page 64) or 1 teaspoon dried

1 cup grated Asiago or similar cheese (omit for vegan version)

Unlike your traditional risotto, this one is whole grain and full of nutrients. It is a delicious variation on the traditional theme. The barley lends itself to creaminess, and as you continue to add liquid, it thickens and softens while maintaining its unique flavor. The mushrooms, leeks, and sun-dried tomatoes each bring an earthy and slightly sweet addition to the flavor mix.

Cook the barley in 3 cups of the stock until it's tender, about 40 minutes. In a large, deep skillet, heat 1/4 cup of the olive oil over medium heat and sauté the garlic for about 2 minutes. Add the barley and slowly add 1 1/2 cups of the milk. Stir constantly over medium heat, adding small amounts of wine, stock, and milk as the barley absorbs the liquid. Keep stirring as it gets creamy. Continue to add liquid as needed for 20 to 25 minutes. The barley should be creamy, not mushy. If you prefer it creamier, continue with the slow cooking and addition of liquid for up to an hour.

THE FAMILY KITCHEN

This is a dish that wants to sit and cook slowly on the stovetop. Put someone in charge of stirring and watching as it gradually cooks into a caramel creation. This is chemistry put into tasty practice. It is fun to keep adding more liquid, knowing that the more it cooks, the better it is. Kids always enjoy cutting the sun-dried tomatoes with scissors too.

In a separate saucepan, heat the remaining 1/4 cup of olive oil over medium heat, add the leeks, mushrooms, sun-dried tomatoes, meat (if using), and thyme. Reduce the heat to low, add the barley risotto to the vegetables, and combine well. Fold in the cheese and mix until well blended, adding more liquid if desired.

Potato and Sweet Pea Croquettes

SERVES 10 TO 12

5 pounds red potatoes, quartered

2 tablespoons olive oil

1 bunch green onions or ramps, chopped

6 cloves garlic, minced

4 cups fresh sweet peas (frozen peas and edamame work too)

2 eggs, beaten

1 cup flour or fine bread crumbs

2 teaspoon salt

1 tablespoon minced fresh thyme (see Growing Green Flavor, page 64) or 1 teaspoon dried

1 tablespoon minced fresh rosemary or 1 teaspoon dried

Vegetable oil for frying

SAUCE:

1 cup yogurt or soft cheese (cream cheese or chèvre work well)

6 tablespoons Dijon or stone-ground mustard

1 cup apple juice

1/4 cup cider vinegar

4 cloves garlic, minced

2 tablespoons minced fresh dill or 2 teaspoons dried

2 teaspoons salt

1/2 to 1 cup milk as needed

These croquettes are very similar to traditional potato pancakes. Of course, the fresh sweet peas give it a bright flavor and a flash of color that make them anything but ordinary. And when the spring pea season is over, you can always use frozen peas and enjoy them as a reminder of springs to come.

Boil the potatoes until they are tender to the fork. Drain the potatoes, mash them, and set them aside.

Heat the olive oil and sauté the onions and garlic, then add the peas. Allow the peas to cook until tender, about two minutes. Puree the pea mixture in a food processor or with an immersion blender. Add the pea mixture to the potatoes, along with the eggs, flour, salt, thyme, and rosemary, and mix well. Form the mixture into patties about 2 inches wide. Fry the patties in hot oil until they're browned on both sides, or put them in an oiled pan and bake them at 350 degrees for about 20 to 25 minutes.

To make the sauce, combine the yogurt, mustard, apple juice, vinegar, garlic, dill, and salt in a small bowl and whisk until creamy. Whisk in as much milk as needed to reach the consistency you like. Serve the sauce with the croquettes.

THE FAMILY KITCHEN

Fresh peas need to be shelled, and the kids will have fun shelling. Just remember to have double what is needed for the recipe, because the sweet treat of raw peas will have the kids slipping open one pod to eat and one pod for the bowl. They can also help form the patties and they will enjoy whisking the sauce.

Baked Tofu and Asparagus with Mixed-Olive Pesto ✻

SERVES 6 TO 8

TOFU:

2 cups apple juice

1/2 cup lemon juice with zest

8 cloves garlic, minced

1/4 cup olive oil

1 cup white wine

2 teaspoons salt or
2 tablespoons tamari

4 pounds tofu, cut into
triangles or rectangles
about 2 inches thick
(about 6 per 1-pound block)

ASPARAGUS:

20 stalks asparagus, trimmed
(see The Family Kitchen,
page 76, for trimming
directions)

3 tablespoons olive oil

3 tablespoons white wine
vinegar

Salt

PESTO:

4 cloves garlic

1 cup walnuts

3 cups mixed olives, pitted

1/2 cup coarsely chopped
fresh basil (see Growing
Green Flavor, page 64)
or 1 tablespoon dried

1/4 cup olive oil (if needed)

*There can never be too many ways to prepare asparagus.
Olives seem to be a nice complement to it, and this recipe is
also a good way to use tofu. Serve this with cooked grains and
a spring-greens salad.*

Preheat the oven to 350 degrees. Whisk together the apple
juice, lemon juice and zest, garlic, olive oil, white wine, and
salt in a bowl. Place the tofu in large sauté pan and pour the
marinade over the tofu. Bring to a boil over medium heat,
then reduce to low heat and simmer, covered, for 15 minutes.
Transfer the tofu to an oiled pan and bake for 20 minutes,
flipping the tofu once to brown both sides.

While the tofu is baking, coat the asparagus with the olive
oil, vinegar, and salt and place it in a baking pan. Roast it for
about 10 minutes, or until bright green and tender. (You could
also grill the tofu and the asparagus until nicely browned.)
Remove the tofu and the asparagus from the oven and allow
them to cool.

To make the pesto, place the garlic, walnuts, olives, and
basil in a food processor and pulse to a coarse paste. With
the machine running, slowly pour in as much olive oil as
needed to create a smooth paste. Serve the pesto over the
tofu and asparagus.

Wild Rice–Almond Croquettes *

MAKES 10 TO 12
CROQUETTES OR
4 TO 6 PATTIES

2 tablespoons olive oil

1 small red onion, minced

2 cloves garlic, minced

3 stalks celery, minced

1 pound tofu

1 cup hand-parched wild rice cooked in 2 cups water (see Wild Rice, page 70)

1 cup toasted almonds, finely chopped (see Toasting Nuts, page 27)

1 tablespoon Dijon or stone-ground mustard

2 teaspoons celery seed

2 tablespoons chopped fresh dill (see Growing Green Flavor, page 64) or 2 teaspoons dried

2 teaspoons salt

2 tablespoons unbleached or brown rice flour (if needed)

As a huge fan of authentic wild rice, I'm thrilled when I find a flavorful and fabulous way to make it the star of a recipe. This recipe is very simple, and the robust flavors combine to make a croquette that deserves main-course attention. Add a green salad and sliced fresh fruit, and dinner is complete.

Preheat the oven to 375 degrees. In a large skillet, heat the olive oil over medium heat and sauté the onion, garlic, and celery until tender and soft, about 5 minutes. Blend the tofu in a food processor until it's creamy.

In a large bowl, combine the sautéed vegetables, tofu, wild rice, almonds, mustard, celery seed, dill, and salt and mix well. The mixture should hold together well, but if it is too wet, add up to 2 tablespoons of flour. Form the mixture into 2-inch balls and bake for 25 minutes on a lightly oiled pan or form 3-inch patties and fry them in a skillet until browned on both sides.

Wild Mushroom Stroganoff over Buckwheat Noodles ✦

SERVES 6 TO 8

Vegetable oil for frying (peanut oil works well because it has a high smoke point)

3 blocks (1¹/₂ pounds) tempeh, cubed

4 tablespoons toasted sesame oil

1¹/₂ to 2 cups coconut milk

1¹/₂ to 2 cups tahini

¹/₄ cup miso paste

²/₃ cup water

2 tablespoons tamari

8 cloves garlic, minced

2 inches ginger, peeled and sliced finely

2 leeks, rinsed and sliced

4 to 5 cups mushrooms (shiitake and cremini work well), sliced about ¹/₄ inch thick

1 cup fresh shelled peas (in a pinch, use peas frozen by a local processor such as Sno Pac)

Homemade buckwheat noodles (recipe follows)

This is not your traditional stroganoff, but has elements that resemble one. The mushrooms are still the centerpiece of the sauce, but they are joined by tempeh and miso, each adding a lightly fermented undertone, and tahini and toasted sesame oil, contributing a nutty flavor. They cream deliciously well together with the coconut milk, resulting in a taste experience that seems both familiar and unheard-of at the same time. The homemade noodles are also very different from typical noodles: their flavor is strong and they are firmer than the store-bought variety. Be sure to allow an hour for the noodles to dry before you boil them. The noodles can be prepared ahead of time and will keep up to four days if they are well wrapped and refrigerated.

Heat the frying oil in a deep-sided pan. Fry the tempeh and set it aside.

To make the sauce, whisk together 2 tablespoons of the sesame oil, coconut milk, tahini, miso paste, water, and tamari and set it aside for now. Sauté the garlic, ginger, and leeks in the remaining 2 tablespoons of sesame oil. Add the mushrooms and peas and sauté for about 2 minutes. Add the

THE FAMILY KITCHEN

The stroganoff works well on, well, nearly anything from potatoes to rice. But the buckwheat noodles make it a celebration. The kids will love making their own noodles. And while the stroganoff is coming together, the kids (young and old) can enjoy rolling and cutting noodles so they can dry before they need to be cooked. In a pinch, Japanese soba noodles will also work as a substitute.

NOODLES:

4 cups light buckwheat flour

3$^{1}/_{4}$ cups wheat flour

2 to 2$^{1}/_{2}$ cups hot water

sauce and stir over medium heat until it is slightly thickened, about 8 to 10 minutes. Serve the sauce over homemade buckwheat noodles. If you don't have time to make noodles, packaged soba noodles, barley, cooked potatoes, or another starch are lovely alternatives.

In a large mixing bowl, blend the flours. While stirring the flour in a circular motion with your hand, pour in 1$^{3}/_{4}$ cups of hot water in a continuous stream, stirring constantly to keep lumps from forming. Continue to mix with your hands until all of the flour is moistened. Using both hands, grasp some damp flour with your fingertips, press it into your palms, and let it drop back into the bowl. Continue to work the dough in this manner until it feels like little pebbles. Gradually add the rest of the water until you can feel the dough starting to take on body. Break apart clumps of dough, let them drop back into the bowl, and repeat. Work the dough until it will form into one big, smooth ball. Continue kneading the dough until it's smooth and elastic, rolling it around inside of the bowl to get rid of hidden air pockets. Divide the dough into 6 equal portions and form each one into a ball. Place them in a bowl and cover it with a damp cloth.

Sprinkle a large work surface with buckwheat flour and roll out a ball of dough until it is about $^{1}/8$ inch thick, 6 inches long, and 3 inches wide. Using a sharp knife, cut the dough into very thin strips. Set them on a baking pan to dry for an hour.

To cook the noodles, bring a large pot of water to a rolling boil, drop in the noodles, and cook them for 2 to 3 minutes. Drain the noodles and serve with the stroganoff.

Savory Chard and Goat Cheese Tart

TWO TARTS SERVE
12 TO 16

CRUST:

$1/3$ cup whole wheat flour

$1/3$ cup unbleached flour

$1/2$ cup cornmeal

$1/4$ cup butter or olive oil

$1/2$ to I cup ice water

FILLING:

$1/4$ cup olive oil

I large or 2 small leeks,
rinsed and sliced

6 cloves garlic, minced

I small red bell pepper,
minced

2 bunches Swiss chard
(or spinach), stemmed and
ripped or chopped into
small pieces

2 tablespoons minced fresh
thyme (see Growing Green
Flavor, page 64) or
2 teaspoons dried

I tablespoon chopped fresh
rosemary or I teaspoon dried

6 eggs

I cup milk, buttermilk,
or yogurt

6 to 8 ounces Montrachet
or chèvre, chilled

This is the kind of dish that is easy to make and works well at the end of a spring day when you're not certain what to make. It can be made ahead to serve at room temperature and works well as part of a brunch or a picnic or as the main course for an elegant yet light evening dinner.

Preheat the oven to 375 degrees and grease two 9-inch tart pans.

In a bowl, mix together the flours and cornmeal for the crust. Cut in the butter until it is evenly distributed. Make a well in the center of the flour mixture, slowly add about $1/2$ cup of ice water, and mix it in with your hands. Add the remaining water a little at a time, using only as much as needed for the dough to form a soft ball. Divide the dough in half and roll out the crusts on a floury surface or between sheets of waxed paper, then gently place them in the tart pans. Press the dough into the pans with your fingers, prick them with a fork, and bake them for about 6 minutes.

> **THE FAMILY KITCHEN**
>
> The kids will love rolling out the crust for the tart while you prepare the filling. Consider doubling the crust recipe and letting the kids have even more fun rolling, cutting, and shaping the extra dough into different shapes. They can make small thumbprint mini tarts to bake on a tray and later fill with a little cheese or jam.

In a large skillet, heat the olive oil and sauté the leeks and garlic for about 3 minutes, then add the red pepper and continue to sauté until it's tender, about 3 more minutes. Add the chard, thyme, and rosemary and sauté just until the chard is wilted. Remove the pan from the heat. Whisk together the eggs and milk in a bowl.

Divide the sautéed vegetable filling between the two crusts, spreading it evenly. Dot each tart evenly with goat cheese, then pour the egg mixture over the filling. Bake until the top is lightly golden, about 30 to 40 minutes. Let the tarts rest for 5 to 10 minutes before cutting them.

Layered Ginger Curry ✴

1 squash, such as butternut or buttercup, peeled, seeded, and sliced in large rounds

3 large carrots, sliced diagonally

3 tablespoons olive oil

2 tablespoons toasted sesame oil

2 large leeks, rinsed and slice

1 to 2 serrano chilies, minced

1/4 cup tamari

1/4 cup rice vinegar

3 tablespoons honey (use agave syrup or maple syrup for vegan version)

4 cloves garlic, minced

2 inches ginger, peeled and minced

2/3 cup coconut milk

3 tablespoons lime juice (about 2 medium limes)

3 tablespoons arrowroot

1/2 cup (about 1/2 bunch) chopped fresh cilantro

1 bunch lacinato kale or collards or spinach, tough stems removed, roughly chopped

1 (16-ounce) package wide, flat rice noodles

This easy-to-make but exotic-tasting dish is the result of experimenting with the notion of a casserole. I think it's a successful break with the traditional Minnesotan idea of a one-pan meal. I like how this dish arranges a mixture of strong Asian influences, from hot chilies to rice vinegar, cilantro, and lime juice. As I learned from my friend Raghavan Iyer, curry simply means "sauce," and as often as not is prepared without turmeric.

Steam the squash and carrots until they are tender but not mushy. In a large skillet, heat 2 tablespoons of olive oil and the sesame oil over medium heat and sauté the leeks for 2 minutes. Add the chilies, squash, and carrots and sauté until soft. In a bowl, combine the tamari, rice vinegar, honey, garlic, ginger, coconut milk, lime juice, and arrowroot. Add the liquid to the squash mixture and simmer on low heat for 3 to 4 minutes. Add the cilantro and remove the pan from the heat. Separate the sauce from the vegetables and save it.

Preheat the oven to 350 degrees. In a large skillet, heat the remaining 1 tablespoon of olive oil, and wilt the greens over medium heat. Soften the noodles in hot water and drain them. In a deep baking pan, layer the ingredients as you would lasagna: sauce, noodles, vegetables, greens; sauce, noodles, vegetables, greens. Bake until heated through, about 20 to 25 minutes.

Smoked Salmon, Asparagus, and Goat Cheese Tart

**TWO TARTS SERVE
12 TO 16**

CRUST:

¹/₃ cup whole wheat pastry flour

¹/₃ cup unbleached flour

¹/₂ cup cornmeal

¹/₄ cup butter or olive oil

¹/₂ to 1 cup ice water

FILLING:

2 tablespoons olive oil

¹/₂ red onion, sliced thinly

¹/₂ pound asparagus, cut into thirds (see **The Family Kitchen**, page 76)

3 cloves garlic, coarsely chopped

4 eggs

1 cup buttermilk

1 tablespoon minced fresh dill (see **Growing Green Flavor**, page 64) or 2 teaspoons dried

1 teaspoon salt

¹/₂ pound smoked salmon, coarsely crumbled

1 small tomato, diced small, or 12 cherry tomatoes, halved

6 ounces Montrachet or chèvre, chilled and crumbled

This combination takes the richest, most beloved flavors in all categories—protein, vegetable, and dairy—and ties them together with a stable egg base. With the hint of cornmeal in the crust, these flavors are over-the-top perfect for each other. Try this at your next party. Cut small pieces or the tart will be gone in seconds.

Preheat the oven to 375 degrees and grease two 10-inch tart pans.

Combine the dry ingredients and cut in the butter until the mixture is crumbly. Slowly add only as much ice water as needed to create a nice doughy texture. The dough should be soft and pliable but not sticky. Divide the dough in half and roll out the crusts on a floury surface or between sheets of waxed paper, then gently flip them into the tart pans. Press the dough into the pans with your fingers, prick them with a fork, and bake them for about 5 to 8 minutes.

Heat the olive oil and sauté the onion for 2 minutes. Add the asparagus and garlic and sauté for 2 to 3 more minutes, until the asparagus is bright green. Remove the pan from the heat.

THE FAMILY KITCHEN

The rich and distinct flavors of this tart might have some kids turning up their noses. One way to make certain even picky eaters are willing to try the delicious final result is to have them whisk the egg and buttermilk into a beautiful golden froth.

(continued)

In a bowl, combine the eggs, buttermilk, dill, and salt and whisk well. Place the baked crusts on a baking sheet. Combine the asparagus mixture and the smoked salmon and spread the mixture in the crusts. Spread the tomatoes and cheese over the salmon and asparagus and gently mix them in. Pour the egg mixture over the filling. Bake the tarts for 20 to 25 minutes. The filling should fluff up some and be nicely browned and firm. If it is not firm, return the tarts to the oven for 5 to 10 more minutes. Let the tarts sit at least 20 minutes before serving.

Falafel

FALAFEL:

1 cup garbanzo beans
(chickpeas) cooked in 3 cups
water (see Cooking Beans
and Legumes, page 7) or
2 cups canned garbanzos

1 onion, coarsely chopped

3 tablespoons coarsely
chopped fresh parsley
(see Growing Green Flavor,
page 64)

3 tablespoons coarsely
chopped fresh cilantro

1 teaspoon salt

2 cloves garlic, minced

1 teaspoon cumin

1 teaspoon baking powder

4 to 6 tablespoons flour

1/2 to 1 cup peanut oil
for frying

TAHINI SAUCE:

1/3 cup tahini

1/4 cup water

1 teaspoon lemon juice

Salt

I fell in love with falafel the first time I tried it and loved it even more on the streets of Israel. For some reason it is unlike any other kind of veggie burger. The garbanzo beans are rich and almost meaty, but carry the strong spices with a lightness that is delightful and satisfying. I prefer peanut oil for frying the falafel. You can heat it to the high temperature needed for a nice crispy falafel fritter without it smoking.

Puree the garbanzo beans and onion in a food processor. Add the parsley, cilantro, salt, garlic, and cumin and process until blended. Sprinkle in the baking powder, and add enough flour so the dough forms a ball and no longer sticks. Add a little water if needed. Form the dough into small balls about the size of donut holes. Heat the peanut oil in a deep, heavy frying pan. Fry the falafel balls on each side until they're golden brown.

To make the tahini sauce, whisk together the tahini, water, and lemon juice. Add salt to taste. Serve the falafel alone or as the quintessential falafel sandwich: a fresh pita filled with falafel, chopped cucumbers, tomatoes, iceberg lettuce, and topped with tahini sauce or your favorite hot sauce.

THE FAMILY KITCHEN

These are another one of those unexpected kid's favorites. As with any recipe where you need to form patties or other shapes, making the little balls is half the fun. Kids will enjoy mixing the tahini sauce and sampling it on the falafel.

Tempeh or Chicken Fajitas ⓥ

SERVES 12 TO 14

Fajitas are a fun, fork-free food that kids and adults can really enjoy. Fajitas lend themselves to a variety of toppings and additions, and are a nice change of pace from the old standby, quesadillas. I find that soy tempeh holds up better and is less crumbly than the mixed-grain varieties. This dish would also work well with mock duck (seitan) or tofu.

MARINADE:

1 cup tamari

2 cups cider vinegar

4 cups tomato puree

5 cups diced tomatoes

1 cup chopped fresh cilantro (see Growing Green Flavor, page 64) or 3 tablespoons ground coriander

3 tablespoons cumin

3 tablespoons chili powder

3 tablespoons garlic powder

3 teaspoons salt

2 cups water

Mix together the tamari, vinegar, tomato puree, diced tomatoes, cilantro, cumin, chili powder, garlic powder, salt, and water. Pour the marinade over the red peppers and tempeh or chicken and marinate for 2 hours, stirring occasionally.

Sauté the onion in oil for 2 to 3 minutes, then add the tempeh or chicken and the red peppers and sauté for another 5 to 7 minutes, until cooked through. Heat the tortillas in a warm pan. To serve, let everyone fill a warmed tortilla with fajita mixture and their choice of toppings.

FILLING:

3 red bell peppers, sliced in 2-inch long strips

3 pounds tempeh, seitan, or chicken breasts, sliced into strips 1½ inches long and ½ inch wide

1 red onion, sliced thinly lengthwise

¼ cup oil

12 to 16 corn or flour tortillas

THE FAMILY KITCHEN

This recipe provides as much fun in the eating as in the preparation. Kids love to get all the condiments ready in anticipation of eating this fun finger food. Try different types of cheeses, salsas, and, of course, guacamole. (For a simple guacamole, use a fork to mash a ripe avocado with just a shot of lime juice and a dash of salt—another great kid task!)

OPTIONAL TOPPINGS:

Grated cheese (or soy alternative)

Sour cream (or soy alternative)

Salsa

Mashed avocado

Chopped lettuce

Sweet corn kernels

Three Sisters Salad ⓥ

SERVES 10 TO 12

Beans, corn, and squash are complementary foods that, eaten together, create a complete protein. Instead of squash, however, I use barley as the foundation for this salad—barley is a wonderful, chewy, and underused grain that is sweet and hearty. The colors and textures of this salad bring out the essence of late summer passing into early autumn.

SALAD:

2 cups corn kernels (cut fresh off the cob or frozen)

1 pound green beans, ends removed and cut into 2-inch pieces

1 pound mustard, baby spinach, or other greens, trimmed and chopped

2 cups pearled barley cooked in 4 cups water (see Cooking Grains, page 48)

1 small red onion, thinly sliced

1 cup sun-dried tomatoes, rehydrated in boiling water and sliced

1/2 pound tempeh or cooked chicken (optional)

In a large saucepan, steam the corn, green beans, and greens in a steamer basket set over water until the colors are bright, about 2 minutes. The beans and corn will be crunchy and sweet. Immediately cool the vegetables under cold water and drain. In a large bowl, combine the barley with the steamed vegetables, onions, sun-dried tomatoes, and tempeh or chicken (if using).

In a separate bowl, whisk together the olive oil, vinegar, mustard, honey, dill, garlic, and salt. Pour half the dressing over the salad and stir to blend. Serve the remaining dressing on the side so people can add more according to individual taste.

DRESSING:

1/2 cup olive oil

1/4 cup cider vinegar

1/4 cup raspberry vinegar

2 tablespoons Dijon or stone-ground mustard

2 tablespoons honey (use agave syrup for vegan version)

1/4 cup fresh dill, chopped, or 2 tablespoons dried

4 cloves garlic, minced

2 teaspoon salt

THE FAMILY KITCHEN

This dish was inspired by the Native American legend about the three sisters: corn, beans, and squash. While the kids trim the ends off the beans, you can discuss how the three "sisters" depended upon each other: the corn offers a natural pole for the beans to climb, the beans feed the corn and squash with nitrogen and other vitamins, and the squash spreads out around them to prevent weeds from growing while its spiny vines keep predators away.

Simple Garlic-Rubbed Salmon and Vegetables with Sweet Basil Dressing

SERVES 4 (8 IF THE STEAKS
ARE DIVIDED)

DRESSING:

1/2 cup olive oil

1/3 cup champagne vinegar

1/4 cup fruity vinegar like
raspberry or currant

1/4 cup orange juice

2 tablespoons honey

1/2 cup mayonnaise

2 cups fresh basil leaves, minced

4 cloves garlic, minced

2 teaspoons salt

SALAD:

1 tablespoon olive oil

6 to 8 cups mixed chopped
seasonal vegetables such as snap
peas, broccoli, cauliflower, and
summer squash

4 cups leafy mixed greens

SALMON:

8 cloves garlic, chopped

4 tablespoons chopped fresh
herbs, such as thyme, rosemary,
and basil (see Growing Green
Flavor, page 64)

1/2 cup olive oil

2 teaspoons salt

4 salmon steaks (preferably wild-
caught salmon from northern
streams or from local fisheries)

This simple marinade for fish is paired with an equally simple dressing for vegetables. They work together nicely and are very versatile. The marinade will work well with almost any type of fish, and the vegetables, too, will complement most any fish. Keep this one in your back pocket for your next spontaneous barbeque.

Make the salad first so it has time to chill. Whisk together the 1/2 cup of olive oil, vinegar, orange juice, honey, mayonnaise, basil, garlic, and salt. In a large skillet, heat the tablespoon of olive oil over medium heat and sauté the vegetables for 5 to 7 minutes. Toss the vegetables with the dressing and put them in the fridge to chill.

Prepare the salmon marinade. Combine the garlic, herbs, olive oil, and salt. Rub or brush the marinade over the salmon steaks. Let the salmon marinate or cook it immediately. Place the salmon steaks directly on an oiled grill grate and cook for about 8 to 10 minutes, turning the salmon after 3 to 5 minutes, depending on how hot your grill is.

Serve the vegetables over a bed of greens alongside the grilled salmon steaks.

Multicolored Potato Gratin with Heirloom Tomato Sauce and Sausage or Tofu Ⓥ

SERVES 10 TO 12

8 medium potatoes in various colors, halved lengthwise if bigger than 1¹⁄₂ inches in diameter, and sliced about ¹⁄₄ inch thick

2 medium red onions, sliced thick

8 tablespoons olive oil

Salt

2 tablespoons honey or brown sugar

2 tablespoons apple cider vinegar

1 to 1¹⁄₂ pounds chicken or pork sausages, chopped (use tofu for vegan version)

1 large onion, chopped

6 cloves garlic, chopped

¹⁄₄ cup sherry vinegar

12 tomatoes (about 3 pounds) (these may vary in size from small to very large), chopped

1 cup tomato paste or puree

¹⁄₄ cup maple syrup

2 cups mushrooms, sliced (optional)

1 to 2 cups soft cheese like queso fresco or gruyere, shredded (omit for vegan option)

Slowly we have become introduced—or rather, reintroduced—to the rainbow range of colors available in heirloom tomatoes and potatoes. When these come into season, I can hardly wait to see all the different possibilities that arrive at the farmers' markets or local marketplace.

Likewise, the art of sausage making is flourishing again. There are numerous local options to choose from. Go to the meat department of your local co-op—many of them have house-made chicken, elk, bison, pork, or beef sausages—or see what some of the local meat vendors at the farmers' market have to offer. Also check the offerings at your local butcher shop. Here in Minneapolis, we're lucky to have Clancy's Butcher Shop in Linden Hills.

Preheat the oven to 400 degrees. Combine the potatoes, sliced red onions, 4 tablespoons (¹⁄₄ cup) of the olive oil, salt, honey, and apple cider vinegar in a shallow baking pan. Roast, stirring often, until tender and caramelized, about 20 to 25 minutes.

While the potatoes are cooking, heat 2 tablespoons of the olive oil in a large pan over medium heat and brown the sausage or the tofu. In a second pan, heat the remaining 2 tablespoons of oil and sauté the chopped onions and garlic.

THE FAMILY KITCHEN

Try a taste test with your kids. Have them close their eyes and see if they can detect any differences in flavor or texture among the different varieties of potatoes or tomatoes. The rainbow is in full bloom at this time of year, enjoy it.

(continued)

Add the sherry vinegar, tomatoes, tomato paste, and maple syrup (also add the mushrooms now if you are including them). Bring to a simmer and allow the sauce to thicken slightly. If it gets too thick, add water a few tablespoons at a time until the sauce is a consistency that will coat a spoon. Add the sausage to the sauce and remove the pan from the heat.

Reduce the oven temperature to 375 degrees. Layer the potato and onion mixture in the bottom of a large baking dish, top with the tomato sauce, and, if desired, sprinkle the cheese over the top. Bake for about 10 to 15 minutes, until heated through and the cheese is melted.

Summer Fried Rice ⓥ

SERVES 10 TO 12

1 tablespoon tamari

1 tablespoon mustard

1 tablespoon maple syrup

¼ cup apple juice

4 eggs (omit for vegan version)

1 tablespoon plus 1 teaspoon toasted sesame oil

1 tablespoon olive oil

1 large yellow or white onion, sliced

2 carrots, sliced fairly thin

4 cloves garlic, minced

1 red bell pepper, sliced

2 cups chopped red or green cabbage

1 large head broccoli, peeled and cut into ½-inch pieces, including 2 inches of the stem

½ head cauliflower, cut into ½-inch pieces

2 cups snap peas or green beans, tips removed and cut in half, or 2 cups fresh sweet peas

2 cups fresh sweet corn kernels

This is a Midwestern crazy quilt of summer vegetables, spread out over a bed of rice or noodles. The understated sauce brings umami—that enigmatic fifth taste described by the Japanese word for "savoriness"—together with sweet from the apple flavor, resulting in a pleasingly juicy blend. The sesame oil adds a touch of Asian flavor to the scrambled eggs. You can make this dish again and again with different vegetables and protein for endless variation. It is light, satisfying, and simple for warm or cool summer evenings on the porch. This dish travels well, so it will be a highlight of a summer family reunion or picnic.

In a small bowl, whisk together the tamari, mustard, maple syrup, and apple juice. Set the bowl aside.

Beat the 4 eggs with a fork in a bowl. In a skillet, heat the teaspoon of sesame oil and scramble the eggs. Set the eggs aside. (For a vegan version, eliminate this step.)

THE FAMILY KITCHEN

With all of the vegetables in this dish, the kids will have a great time chopping and sorting for preparation. I recommend that you get plenty of sweet corn and have them cut off kernels (this can be done with a butter knife) above and beyond what's needed in the recipe. Break the cobs in half so they are more manageable. They'll enjoy discovering how sweet and delicious corn is even without being cooked, and you can put the extra in the fridge to toss into future stir-fries, soups, or salads.

(continued)

2 cups brown rice cooked in 4 cups water (see Cooking Grains, page 64) or 4 cups rice noodles softened in hot water and drained

1 pound protein such as diced cooked chicken breast or browned tofu, tempeh, or mock duck (optional)

1/2 cup coarsely chopped toasted almonds or cashews (optional)

Heat the olive oil and remaining tablespoon of sesame oil in a large saucepan or a wok. When the oil is hot, add the onions and carrots and sauté about 3 minutes. Turn the heat down to medium and add the garlic, bell pepper, cabbage, broccoli, and cauliflower and sauté for another 5 minutes. Then add the peas, corn, scrambled eggs, and tamari mixture and cook until peas and corn are steamed, about 1 to 2 minutes. Remove from the heat and serve over rice or noodles. Top with the protein and nuts, if desired.

Wild Mushroom and Tuna Casserole

SERVES 8 TO 12

5 tablespoons olive oil

3 leeks, rinsed and sliced

1 pound wild mushrooms such as shiitake or cremini, sliced (about 4 cups)

1 pound green beans or snap peas

6 cloves garlic, minced

2 teaspoons salt

1 tablespoon minced fresh thyme or 1½ teaspoons dried

1 tablespoon celery seed

1 cup Kalamata olives, pitted and chopped

1½ pounds tuna, sliced into small pieces

2 cups milk or soymilk

2 tablespoons flour

½ cup cheese such as a soft cheddar (optional)

This dish bears no resemblance to the tuna casserole you likely ate in the school cafeteria. With the deep flavor of the mushrooms and the bright taste of the olives and peas, the familiar dish of your youth is all grown up.

Preheat the oven to 350 degrees. Heat 2 tablespoons of the olive oil in a heavy skillet over medium heat and sauté 2 of the leeks. After 3 to 4 minutes, add the mushrooms, green beans, garlic, salt, thyme, and celery seed. Sauté until nicely softened, about five minutes, then remove the pan from the heat, add the olives, and transfer the contents to a baking dish.

Whisk together the milk and flour. In a heavy skillet over medium heat, sauté the tuna pieces in 2 more tablespoons of the olive oil, add the milk and flour mixture, and stir until thickened, about 2 or 3 minutes. Tuna gets tough and overcooked quickly, so just heat it through and then remove the pan from the heat. It is fine to have some pink showing. Fold the tuna into the vegetable mixture in the baking dish.

In a heavy skillet over medium heat, sauté the remaining leek in the remaining tablespoon of olive oil until it's very crispy. Remove from the heat and sprinkle over the casserole along with the crumbled or grated cheese, if desired. Bake until heated through, about 10 to 15 minutes.

THE FAMILY KITCHEN

While many of our kids may not be familiar with that old tuna casserole of our youth, this will have the same appeal with its creamy sauce, yummy peas, and crispy fried onions on top. They can help to assemble the dish and taste and smell the real versions of stuff we used to get from a can.

Seafood Kebabs in Lime–Ginger Marinade ⓥ

MAKES 18 LARGE KEBABS

MARINADE:

3 inches ginger, peeled and chopped fine

6 cloves garlic, minced

2 cups orange juice (about 6 medium oranges)

1 cup honey (use rice syrup or maple syrup for vegan version)

2 cups lime juice (about 16 medium limes)

¹/₂ cup rice vinegar

KEBABS:

10 to 12 cups of your choice of proteins and vegetables cut into 1-inch cubes (possibilities include catfish, tilapia, or salmon; mock duck or tempeh; eggplant, bell peppers, zucchini, cherry tomatoes, mushrooms, and red onion)

This marinade works wells on a variety of proteins and vegetables. It is light and snappy, works especially well with fish, and is great for grilling. It is totally refreshing on a warm summer evening, and will be especially enjoyed by guests dining outside on the porch or in the backyard.

To make the marinade, simmer the ginger and garlic in the orange juice and honey in a saucepan over low heat for 10 minutes. Remove from the heat and stir in the lime juice and vinegar.

Assemble the kebabs. I suggest using 10- or even 12-inch skewers and placing five or six pieces on each one, which guarantees a good-sized kebab that you can easily handle on the grill and also makes for easier eating once off the grill. Place the kebabs in a deep pan and pour the marinade over them. Marinate several hours in the refrigerator, or overnight if possible. The kebabs can be baked in a 385 degree oven for 20 minutes, but are most spectacular when cooked on the grill until well charred, turning often, about 9 minutes.

THE FAMILY KITCHEN

Kids will enjoy skewering the vegtables and fish for these kebabs, but be sure to warn them of potential finger pokes (and they will happen). The combination of honey and lime is a popular one with the kids. Once they lick it off their fingers, they will be tempted to taste it off the grill.

Although baking is intimidating for many people, I have found that **THERE IS A BASIC FORMULA FOR MOST THINGS**, and that having an understanding of this formula really helps—as is true in all cooking. Each mixture is, more or less, a combination of fat, sweetener, leavening, and grain. **FROM THERE, IT IS REALLY A MATTER OF THEME, VARIATION, AND SEASON**. Because I use mostly whole grain flours and liquid sweeteners, these baked goods tend to be fairly dense and moist. If you are aiming for something drier and fluffier, you can use sugar for your sweetener and add another egg for fluffiness.

Basic Whole Wheat Muffins

MAKES 12 MUFFINS

4 cups whole wheat flour
(can substitute about 1 cup
unbleached flour or other
grains like cornmeal, rolled
oats, or ground flax seed)

2 teaspoons baking powder

2 teaspoons baking soda

¹/₂ cup softened butter or oil

2 eggs

1 cup sweetener (honey,
maple syrup, fruit jam,
applesauce, sugar, or a
mixture)

1 teaspoon vanilla extract
(if using almonds, substitute
almond extract; use other
flavors like lemon or maple
for added flavor)

1 to 2 cups apple juice or milk
of your choice

1 cup fruit such as blueberries,
diced apples, or diced
peaches (optional)

1 cup chopped nuts, seeds, or
shredded coconut (optional)

*This is a great base recipe for muffins. You can use this and then
have fun trying different ingredients for variety, texture, and
flavor. To sweeten the muffins, I generally like a combination of
maple syrup and fruit or fruit and sugar. This keeps the batter
moist and brings a balance of strong and fruity sweetness. If you
use only sugar, this will greatly reduce the amount of liquid in the
batter, and you will need to compensate for this when you add
the juice at the end.*

Preheat the oven to 350 degrees. Grease a muffin tin.

Place the flour, baking powder, and baking soda in a bowl
and stir with a fork or a whisk to combine. In another bowl,
stir together the butter, eggs, sweetener, and vanilla extract.
Add the flour mixture to the egg mixture and stir just until

> **THE FAMILY KITCHEN**
>
> Each of my kids has a mini muffin pan and mixing
> bowl. When we make muffins, they each prepare a mini
> version of this recipe (I make the full recipe but also put
> about one-quarter of the amount of each ingredient in
> their bowls too). They mix it and then spoon it into their
> muffin pans. The excitement of seeing their batter turn
> into perfect little muffins is wonderful. They usually
> finish off their entire batch by the end of the day.

(continued)

blended. Add as much of the apple juice or milk as needed to make the batter creamy, slightly sticky, and wet, but not too thin. Stir in any fruit and nuts you are using.

Spoon the batter into the oiled muffin pans and bake for 15 to 20 minutes.

 Variations:

Banana–Cranberry Muffins

Although bananas are never local in the Midwest, they are a great ingredient in baked goods, very popular with kids, and a good source of vitamins and nutrients. I try to buy local, seasonal foods, but bananas are an exception I make throughout the year. Local fresh cranberries start to appear in stores in autumn, which makes them a great choice after other berries are out of season. If you use dried cranberries, choose unsweetened berries.

Use 1 cup of coarsely chopped fresh or frozen cranberries and 2 mashed bananas and add less liquid to the batter.

Blueberry–Cashew Muffins

Be sure to drain the liquid from the blueberries and add them last so they don't turn the muffins blue. Use 1 cup of blueberries and 1 cup of coarsely chopped toasted cashews.

Squash–Pecan Muffins

Use 2 cups of cooked, mashed squash and add less liquid to the batter to compensate for the moisture in the squash. Add 1 cup of toasted chopped pecans and 1 teaspoon each of cinnamon and nutmeg.

Strawberry Cornmeal Muffins

Substitute 1 cup of cornmeal for 1 cup of the flour. You may need to add a little extra liquid to compensate. Gently stir in 1 cup of sliced strawberries at the very end, after the batter is well mixed.

Lemon–Poppy Seed Muffins

Add 1 cup of poppy seeds, $^1/_4$ cup of lemon juice, and the grated zest of 1 lemon.

AS WITH MUFFINS, *once you get a good formula, variations are simply a matter of making a few simple changes or additions to the basic recipe. While there definitely is chemistry involved in baking, and many things such as air temperature, humidity, and flour texture can affect the final product, there is still a basic method.* **THE BEAUTIFUL THING ABOUT THIS SIMPLE METHOD** *is that a little extra of one quality ingredient or a little less of another is not going to ruin the result, it will simply change it.*

Lemon-Poppy Seed Scones

MAKES 8 SCONES

4½ cups pastry flour

2 tablespoons baking powder

1½ teaspoons salt

⅔ cup fruit-sweetened jam or maple syrup

½ cup oil or softened butter (use oil for vegan version)

1 cup poppy seeds

¼ cup lemon zest

¼ cup lemon juice

1 teaspoon lemon extract (optional)

½ cup fruit juice

½ cup buttermilk or yogurt (use soy milk for vegan version)

Preheat the oven to 375 degrees. Grease a baking sheet or line it with parchment paper. Place the flour, baking powder, and salt in a bowl and use a whisk or a fork to combine them. In another bowl, mix together the jam, oil, poppy seeds, lemon zest, lemon juice, lemon extract (if using), fruit juice, and buttermilk. Add the wet ingredients to the flour mixture and stir well. The dough should be soft but not sticky.

Place the dough on a floured surface or a sheet of waxed paper and roll or press it out to form a circle about ½ inch thick. Cut the dough into 8 triangles (like a pizza). Place the triangles on the prepared baking sheet and bake for 12 to 15 minutes.

> ### THE FAMILY KITCHEN
>
> Kids will take great interest in rolling and shaping the scones. Let them choose the fruits or nuts to put inside, and give them a small lump of dough and let them form their own freeform scones. Ultimately the shape doesn't matter—the scones will taste yummy whether they are perfectly shaped or not.

(continued)

Variations:

Blackberry–Coconut Scones
Substitute 1 cup of grated coconut for the poppy seeds and fold
in 1 cup of blackberries at the end.

Date or Currant Walnut Scones
Substitute 1 cup of chopped walnuts for the poppy seeds and
fold in 1 cup of chopped dates or currants at the end.

Apricot–Almond Scones
Substitute 1 cup of chopped toasted almonds for the poppy
seeds and stir in 1 cup of chopped dried apricots.

Apple–Pecan Scones
Substitute 1 cup of chopped toasted pecans for the poppy seeds
and stir in 1 cup of chopped apples (peeled if desired) and 1
teaspoon of cinnamon.

Herbed Crackers

MAKES 2 LARGE SHEETS
OR ABOUT 6 DOZEN
2-INCH SQUARES

1¹/₂ cups whole wheat flour

1 cup unbleached flour

1 cup cornmeal

2 tablespoons minced fresh
thyme or 1 tablespoon dried

2 tablespoons fresh rosemary,
minced or 1 tablespoon dried

1 tablespoon salt

¹/₄ cup ground flax seed
(optional)

3/4 cup butter

¹/₂ to 1 cup cold water

A number of dishes are enhanced when served with something crunchy. And, of course, a little cheese with home-baked crackers is a perfect snack or accompaniment to wine or beer. These crackers are simple and easy to make.

Preheat the oven to 385 degrees and grease a baking sheet. Combine the flours, cornmeal, thyme, rosemary, salt, and flax seed (if using). Cut in the butter with a pastry knife until the dough is well blended and crumbly. Add the cold water slowly until the dough is doughy and pliable but not sticky.

Divide the dough into about 6 pieces and roll them out one at a time on a floured surface. Crackers should be fairly thin, no more than ¹/8 inch thick. Score the crackers into whatever shape you wish, being careful not to cut all the way through the dough. Place them on the oiled baking sheet and prick them well with a fork. Bake for about 8 minutes on one side, turn the crackers over, and bake for another 4 minutes.

Another option is to bake these in large pieces. Divide the dough into 2 portions instead of 6 and roll out each piece of dough to roughly 9×16 inches. Break the crackers into smaller pieces after they have cooled. This is a lovely and organic look and looks great on a buffet.

THE FAMILY KITCHEN

Kids will be thrilled to discover they can make their own crackers and that they're even better than crackers out of a box. They can use a knife or cookie cutters to make different shapes after rolling out the dough.

Wild Rice Crackers *

2 tablespoons yeast

1¹/2 cups warm water

2 teaspoons dill

2 teaspoons garlic powder

2 cups whole wheat flour

1 cup unbleached flour

¹/2 cup cornmeal

¹/2 cup cooked wild rice, ground in a food processor (See Wild Rice, page 70)

1 teaspoon salt

Toasted sesame seeds (optional)

In a large bowl, add the yeast to the warm water. Let the bowl sit until the yeast bubbles, about 5 minutes. Add the dill and garlic powder (these can be omitted for a plain cracker). In another bowl, stir together the flours, cornmeal, wild rice, and salt. Add the flour mixture to the yeast mix. Mix well until the dough is pliable but not sticky. Place the dough in an oiled bowl, cover it, and let the dough rise for about 1 hour. Punch down the dough and let it rest for another 15 to 20 minutes.

Preheat the oven to 400 degrees and grease a baking sheet. Divide the dough into 8 pieces. Working on a floured surface, use a rolling pin to roll out each piece into a very thin round not thicker than ¹/8 inch and about 8 or 9 inches in diameter. Place the rounds on an oiled pan, sprinkle them with the sesame seeds (if desired), and bake for 5 to 6 minutes, until bubbly and browned. When cool, break the rounds into various-sized pieces.

Granola

SERVES 12 TO 14

1 cup oil (coconut oil and canola oil are good options)

1 cup maple syrup

1 tablespoon vanilla

10 cups regular rolled oats

2 cups shredded coconut

2 cups toasted chopped nuts

2 cups flax seed

2 cups dried fruit

There is nothing like homemade granola. As with salad dressing or pie crust, once you make your own, nothing can compare, and you may never go back. This is a simple recipe and there is room for all kinds of variation. You can adjust the quantity of liquid depending on how crunchy or gooey you like your granola and adjust the baking time depending on how toasted you want the granola to be. Also add various nuts, seeds, or dried fruits for infinite flavors.

Preheat the oven to 350 degrees. Combine the oil, maple syrup, and vanilla in a saucepan over medium heat and heat until viscous, about 5 minutes. In a large bowl, combine the rolled oats, coconut, nuts, and flax seed. Pour the syrup over the oat mixture and stir until well coated; the mixture should be moist but not wet.

Spread the granola on a baking pan and bake for about 20 to 25 minutes, stirring frequently so the top layer and edges do not burn. The granola should have a lovely golden color throughout. Remove from the oven when the granola is brown and mix in any dried fruit you are using. Let the granola cool completely, then store it in an airtight container. You can also freeze it in a heavy-duty zipper bag.

THE FAMILY KITCHEN

A recipe like this can provide a great learning opportunity for kids. They get to see that the foods they thought came only from a store or a box are really a simple combination of basic ingredients, and that they have a choice about whether or not to create their own. In addition, as with most of my recipes, kids are empowered to think creatively about texture, flavor, and even aesthetics. Best of all, there is nothing like fresh, warm granola right out of the oven!

Maple Corn Bread

SERVES 8 TO 10

2 cups whole wheat flour

2 cups cornmeal (I use cornmeal from Riverbend Farm or Whole Grain Milling, another fabulous family-owned and sustainable farm located in southwestern Minnesota)

1 tablespoon baking powder

2 teaspoons salt

1 cup vanilla or plain full-fat yogurt (my current favorite is from the Kickapoo region of Wisconsin and has perhaps the best name ever: Cultural Revolution)

1/2 cup pure maple syrup

1/2 cup milk of your choice

1 cup water

This is the moistest, richest corn bread I've made. It is almost cakelike, which is probably why kids and adults love it so much. The honey butter condiment doesn't hurt either. That it's so easy to make is an added bonus.

Preheat the oven to 350 degrees and grease an 8-inch square pan. Combine the flour and cornmeal in a bowl, then add the baking powder and salt and mix well. Add the yogurt and maple syrup and mix again. Then stir in the milk and water until the batter is a thin, spreadable consistency. It is okay if it is fairly thin, as the cornmeal will absorb the water and thicken up. Spread the batter in the prepared pan and bake until the corn bread is firm to the touch, about 20 to 25 minutes.

THE FAMILY KITCHEN

Kids love to help mix, and mixing is even more fun when what they are preparing is honey butter. Just mix a few teaspoons of honey with 1/4 cup of softened butter. Local is best, of course. I use Hope Creamery butter and Ames Farm honey.

Pumpkin Corn Bread

||||||||||||||||||||||||||||||||||||||||||||||||||||||||||||||||||||||||||||||||||||||||||||||||||||||||||||||||||||||||||||

SERVES 8 TO 10

6 tablespoons butter, softened, or oil

¼ cup honey

2 tablespoons molasses

1 cup cooked, pureed pumpkin (canned is fine)

1 cup buttermilk or yogurt

2 eggs

2 to 2½ cups cornmeal

1 to 1½ cups whole wheat pastry flour

1 tablespoon baking powder

1 teaspoon cinnamon

1 teaspoon nutmeg

2 teaspoons salt

1 cup milk or water (approximately)

This recipe is a variation of the maple corn bread so it has that same cakelike appeal but with the added seasonal component of pumpkin, which makes it a perfect companion to any of the soups, and especially with chili (see pages 42 or 47). You can also use other winter squash in place of the pumpkin. The batter is very dense and bakes up moist and flavorful. If you're looking for a lighter texture, stir up to 1 cup of juice or milk into the batter. This corn bread also looks wonderful when baked in an 8-inch cast-iron skillet.

Preheat the oven to 350 degrees. Grease two loaf pans or an 8-inch round cake pan. Combine the butter, honey, molasses, and pumpkin and cream well. Whisk in the buttermilk and eggs. In a separate bowl, combine the cornmeal, flour, baking powder, cinnamon, nutmeg, and salt. Add the flour mixture to the wet mixture and stir until all of the flour is incorporated, adding up to 1 cup of milk or water as needed to create a moist batter. Pour the batter into the prepared pan(s) and bake for 20 to 25 minutes.

Banana Bread *

SERVES 8 TO 10

2 ripe bananas, mashed well

1½ cups fruit jam or maple syrup

2 teaspoons vanilla

1 cup berries or nuts (optional)

4 cups flour (3 cups whole wheat and 1 cup unbleached is a good mix)

1 tablespoon baking powder

1 teaspoon salt

1 to 2 cups apple juice or orange juice

What else are you going to do with over-ripened bananas? While bananas will never be a seasonal treat in this part of the world, they are a reliable kid pleaser as well as a solid package of nutrients and energy.

Preheat the oven to 375 degrees and grease two loaf pans or a 9×13-inch baking pan. In one bowl, mix together the bananas, jam or syrup, vanilla, and nuts (if using). In another bowl, blend the flour, baking powder, and salt. Add the flour mixture to the banana mixture and blend well. Slowly stir in the juice. Pour the batter into the prepared pan(s) and bake for 25 to 30 minutes.

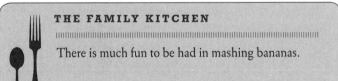

THE FAMILY KITCHEN

There is much fun to be had in mashing bananas.

Fruit Crisp ❦

SERVES 10 TO 12

1½ cups apple juice or cider

10 cups mixed fruit such as apples, peaches, pears, and even berries

1 tablespoon vanilla

3½ cups regular rolled oats

½ cup butter or oil (use oil for vegan version)

3 to 4 cups whole wheat pastry flour

1 teaspoon salt

1 teaspoon cinnamon

Almost any fruit can be made into a flavorful crisp. It's an easy way to create a light and colorful finish to any meal. This is great served with a dollop of freshly whipped Cedar Summit Farm cream. This crisp is also so simple and wholesome that in our house we eat it as breakfast with a scoop of yogurt.

In a saucepan over low heat, heat 1 cup of the juice, the fruit, and the vanilla. Start with the chopped apples or stone fruits and simmer them for 5 to 10 minutes. If you're using berries, add these now and continue to simmer on very low heat for another 10 minutes, until the fruit is very thick and sweet smelling.

Preheat the oven to 375 degrees. While the filling cooks, combine the oats, butter or oil, remaining ½ cup of juice, flour, salt, and cinnamon in a bowl. The dough should be moist, but still slightly crumbly. If it is too wet, add more oats, and if it is too dry, add more liquid. Pour the fruit into a 9×13-inch baking pan and sprinkle the topping on top of the fruit. Cover the pan with foil and bake for about 20 minutes. Remove the foil and bake another 5 to 10 minutes until browned.

THE FAMILY KITCHEN

In Minnesota, berry season is exciting and brief. Families can make an outing to a local u-pick berry farm and pick enough to freeze for later. You can also find berries at the farmers' market or add some plants to your garden. Kids love running out to the garden in their jammies and picking fresh berries for breakfast—it can, however, be tough to save enough for the freezer! There are also great opportunities to go apple picking in the fall.

Carrot Cake Three Ways

SERVES 12 TO 14

3/4 cup oil or butter (use oil for a vegan version)

2 cups maple syrup or 1 cup maple syrup and 1 cup brown sugar

4 cups grated or ground carrots

1 tablespoon vanilla

2 teaspoons cinnamon

2 teaspoons nutmeg

5 to 6 cups pastry flour

2 tablespoons baking powder

1 to 2 cups milk of your choice (use a milk alternative for vegan version)

1½ cups currants

1½ cups chopped walnuts or pecans (optional)

Carrot cake is probably one of the most classic and enduring desserts from the hippie vegetarian era. It never seems to go out of style and is always a wholesome, yet satisfying, sweet. You can make it more or less rich, depending on the topping you choose.

Preheat the oven to 350 degrees. Grease two 9-inch round cake pans or a Bundt pan. In a large bowl, stir together the oil, maple syrup, carrots, vanilla, cinnamon, and nutmeg. In another bowl, whisk together the flour and baking powder. Add the flour mixture to the carrot mixture and mix well. Add only as much milk as needed to make a batter that is smooth and pourable but not thin. Stir in the currants and nuts (if using). Pour the batter into the prepared pan(s). Bake for 30 to 35 minutes, until a knife inserted in the center of the cake comes out clean. Cook the cake on a rack for about 10 minutes, then remove it from the pan. You can glaze a warm cake; for a frosted cake, allow the cake to cool completely.

> **THE FAMILY KITCHEN**
>
> Seeing vegetables transformed into dessert brings a whole new way of thinking about food. When kids help with grating and mixing, and then enjoy the results, their understanding of baking, and food in general, expands. Try preparing more than one of the frostings and do a taste comparison.

ORANGE GLAZE: Ⓥ

¹/₂ cup maple syrup

1 tablespoon vanilla

1 cup orange juice

3 tablespoons arrowroot powder

MAPLE NUT FROSTING: Ⓥ

¹/₂ cup nut butter (my favorites are cashew and almond)

1 pound firm tofu

¹/₃ cup maple syrup

2 teaspoons vanilla

2 tablespoons rice, soy, or cow milk, if needed

CREAM CHEESE FROSTING:

1 cup (¹/₂ pound) unsalted butter, softened

¹/₂ cup maple syrup

2¹/₂ cups (1¹/₄ pounds) cream cheese or Neufchatel cheese, softened

1 tablespoon vanilla

Orange Glaze:

In a saucepan, cook the maple syrup, vanilla, and orange juice over medium heat until warmed through. Remove ¹/₄ cup of this mixture from the saucepan and whisk in the arrowroot powder. Once the arrowroot is completely dissolved, return the mixture to the saucepan while whisking. After the glaze thickens, remove the pan from the heat. Allow the glaze to cool before frosting a layer cake or drizzle the warm glaze over a Bundt cake immediately after removing it from the pan.

Maple Nut Frosting:

Puree all of the ingredients in a food processor until very creamy. If the frosting is too thick, add milk as needed. Chill before using.

Cream Cheese Frosting:

Blend all of the ingredients in a food processor until very creamy. Chill before frosting.

Flourless Chocolate Torte

SERVES 10 TO 12

CAKE:

8 ounces unsweetened baking chocolate

¼ cup butter

1⅓ cups sugar (or ⅔ cup brown sugar and ⅔ cup fruit preserves or maple syrup)

3 eggs, beaten

4 cups finely ground nuts (almonds, hazelnuts, and pecans are favorites)

Grated zest of 1 orange

1 tablespoon vanilla or almond extract

CHOCOLATE GLAZE:

½ cup semisweet chocolate chips

¼ cup unsalted butter

This torte is rich and light at the same time. It is moist in the middle and slightly crispy around the edges. This is perfect for people who can't have wheat or gluten. It is truly a decadent and satisfying dessert. Try it with fresh whipped cream or Cedar Summit Vanilla Ice Cream and you will find yourself in dessert heaven.

Preheat the oven to 375 degrees. Grease an 8-inch springform pan. In a large saucepan or a double boiler, melt the chocolate and butter. Add the sugar, eggs, nuts, orange zest, and vanilla or almond extract and mix well. Spread the batter evenly in the prepared pan and bake for about 30 minutes. The cake should be firm to the touch and pull slightly away from the edges of the pan.

To make the glaze, melt the chocolate chips and butter over low heat in a saucepan or a double boiler. Whisk until well blended. Pour the glaze over the torte while it is still in the springform pan. Place the cake in the freezer to firm up. This cake is best when served chilled. For an added twist, gently stir 1 cup of fresh raspberries or sliced strawberries into the glaze just before pouring it over the cake. Garnish the cake with additional fresh berries before serving.

THE FAMILY KITCHEN

This is yet another chemistry lesson for kids. It is fascinating to learn that you can make a delicious and successful cake without adding any flour! The nuts make up the bulk of this cake and create a delicious, moist, and dense cake.

Nut Butter–Chocolate Chip Cookies ⓥ

MAKES 2 DOZEN

½ cup oil or butter (use oil for vegan version)

1 cup maple syrup or ½ cup maple syrup and ½ cup sugar

1 cup nut butter, either almond or cashew

½ tablespoon vanilla

3½ cups pastry flour

2 teaspoons baking soda

1 teaspoon salt

1½ cups chocolate chips (check that the chocolate does not have added whey, milk fat, or casein for vegan version)

I am a cookie fanatic. I love them fresh out of the oven, so rarely do I bake more than I can eat at one time (I won't say how many that is). I also like to keep them simple, and find that ever since developing these recipes, which are mostly eggless and maple syrup–sweetened, my tastes have changed; standard crunchy cookies made with butter and sugar no longer suffice. My cookies are dense and moist—cookie qualities that I love and, hopefully, you will too.

Preheat the oven to 350 degrees. Grease a cookie sheet.

Stir together the oil, maple syrup, nut butter, and vanilla. In another bowl, whisk together the flour, baking soda, and salt. Add the flour mixture to the wet ingredients and stir to combine. Stir in the chocolate chips. Drop spoonfuls of the dough onto the prepared pan and flatten them with the palm of your hand. Bake 8 to 10 minutes.

> **THE FAMILY KITCHEN**
>
> It is easy to get kids to take part in making these treats. Almost all of these recipes involve hand rolling and pressing, which is always fun for little hands. Let's face it, there are few things better than making cookies together, except maybe licking the bowl afterward. Note: If you want to be frugal, you can extend these recipes to 3 dozen by making the cookies slightly smaller.

Ginger Molasses Cookies

MAKES 2 DOZEN

1/2 cup butter or oil

2 cups maple syrup

1/2 cup molasses

2 eggs

1 1/2 cups coconut (optional)

6 cups pastry flour

1 tablespoon cinnamon

1 tablespoon ginger powder
or 2 tablespoons fresh
minced ginger

2 teaspoons baking soda

1 teaspoon salt

These are a slightly soft version of the classic cookie. The familiar combination of molasses and spices is comforting and just right with a glass of hot cider on a cool fall evening.

Preheat the oven to 350 degrees and grease a baking sheet.

Combine the butter, maple syrup, molasses, and eggs in a large bowl and stir until well blended. If you're using coconut, blend it into this mixture. In a separate bowl, mix together the flour, cinnamon, ginger, baking soda, and salt. Add the flour mixture to the wet ingredients and stir until well incorporated. If the mixture seems too wet, add a little more flour. It should be easy to pull off generous spoon-sized portions and roll them into balls. Place the balls on the prepared pan. Bake for 12 to 15 minutes.

Coco Loco Cookies ⓥ

MAKES 2 DOZEN

1/3 cup butter or oil (use oil for vegan option)

1²/3 cups honey or maple syrup (use maple syrup for vegan option)

2 teaspoons vanilla

1 cup unsweetened cocoa powder

3 to 3¹/3 cups flour

2 teaspoons baking soda

1¹/2 cups shredded coconut

1¹/2 cups chocolate chips (check that the chocolate does not have added whey, milk fat, or casein for vegan version)

When I discovered the chocolate–coconut combination, I tried to think of as many possible ways to put them together as I could. This simple cookie is a double treat because it combines both cocoa powder and chocolate chips with chewy, nutty coconut. I use finely shredded coconut.

Preheat the oven to 350 degrees and grease a baking sheet.

Combine the butter, honey, vanilla, and cocoa powder and beat until creamy. Whisk together the flour and baking soda, then stir the flour mixture into the dough. Stir in the coconut and chocolate chips. Scoop up large spoonfuls of the dough, roll them into balls, and place them on the prepared baking pan. Bake for about 10 minutes.

Oatmeal Raisin Cookies

MAKES 2 DOZEN

1/2 cup butter or oil

1 1/3 cups maple syrup

1 teaspoon vanilla

1 egg

3/4 cup raisins (or chopped dates)

3/4 cup walnuts or pecans, chopped (optional)

2 2/3 cups regular rolled oats

3 cups pastry flour

2 teaspoons baking soda

This is another classic cookie I've tweaked by using maple syrup instead of sugar. The maple syrup balances the raisins and oats for a cookie that is almost good enough for breakfast.

Preheat the oven to 350 degrees and grease a baking sheet.

In a large bowl, stir together the butter, maple syrup, vanilla, and egg, then mix in the raisins and nuts. In a separate bowl, combine the oats, flour, and baking soda. Stir the oat mixture into the wet dough. Scoop up large spoonfuls of the dough, roll them into balls, and place them on the prepared baking pan. Bake for about 12 minutes.

Poppy Seed Cookies ⓥ

MAKES 2 DOZEN

2¹/₂ cups oats, processed in a food processor until fine

3 cups pastry flour

¹/₂ cup poppy seeds

1 teaspoon baking soda

¹/₂ teaspoon salt

1 cup maple syrup

1 cup butter or oil (use oil for vegan version)

2 teaspoons vanilla

2 teaspoons rice vinegar

Just like muffins and scones, cookies are a variation on a theme that highlights whatever flavors you want to combine. I usually try to find a subtle enhancement to an otherwise familiar flavor. In this case, the rice vinegar adds a surprising tang to this shortbread-like cookie.

Preheat the oven to 350 degrees and grease a baking sheet.

In a bowl, whisk together the oats, flour, poppy seeds, baking soda, and salt. In another large bowl, beat the maple syrup, butter, vanilla, and rice vinegar. Mix the oat mixture into the syrup mixture. Scoop up large spoonfuls of the dough, roll them into balls, and place them on the prepared baking pan. Flatten the balls of dough with the palm of your hand. Bake for about 10 minutes.

Cornmeal–Walnut Shortbread

MAKES 2 DOZEN

2 cups (1 pound) unsalted
butter, softened

1 cup maple syrup

1 teaspoon vanilla

3 cups whole wheat
pastry flour

2 to 3 cups cornmeal

1 teaspoon salt

1/2 cup walnuts, finely
chopped

*These cookies were born out of my love for Greg Reynolds's
cornmeal. I keep trying to think of new ways to use it. The
shortbread is not dissimilar to the maple corn bread recipe—this
is just a cookie version. The walnuts add a great crunch and
slight bitterness to balance the sweetness of the corn and maple
syrup. Try this with other nuts for yummy variations.*

Preheat the oven to 350 degrees. Grease a baking sheet or line
it with a silicone pan liner.

Cream together the butter, maple syrup, and vanilla. Add
the pastry flour, 2 cups of the cornmeal, and the salt. Mix until
well combined. The dough should be soft but not sticky. If
it is too sticky, add more cornmeal, 1/4 cup at a time. Gently
incorporate the walnuts into the dough. Put the dough on a
floured surface and roll it into a log about 15 inches long and
1 1/2 inches in diameter. With a sharp knife, cut slices about
1/2 inch thick. Lay the slices on the pan. The cookies will not
spread, so you can place them fairly close together. Bake until
slightly browned and firm, about 15 minutes.

Almond Butter Balls ❋

MAKES 2 DOZEN

2 cups almond butter, cashew butter, or other nut butter

1 cup maple syrup

1 cup rolled oats

1 cup wheat bran or oat bran

1 teaspoon salt

1 cup raisins or other dried fruit (optional)

These simple, healthy treats satisfy the sweet tooth without being too sugary. Any nut butter will work, and you can play around with other ingredients depending on the occasion. For example, use dried cranberries for the holidays or chocolate chips for a really decadent version.

Combine all of the ingredients in a bowl until well mixed. The mixture should be firm enough to roll into balls. If it's not, add more bran. Roll the dough into 1-inch balls, set them on waxed paper, and place them in the fridge or freezer until they're firm, about 1 hour.

THE FAMILY KITCHEN

These cookies can be prepared entirely by kids. They can measure all the ingredients, mix them together, and, best of all, roll them into balls. The size and shape of the balls is open to interpretation.

THERE'S JUST SOMETHING ABOUT BARS—*for some reason they are more special than cookies. Maybe it is because they are thick and cakey. Maybe it's because they are prepared in a pan, which seems to indicate that they are special. While I think the formula for bars is quite similar to that for cookies,* **THESE THREE RECIPES ARE UNIQUE** *and can fancy up a dinner party or other special occasion.*

Apricot–Date Bars

SERVES 18 TO 24

1¹/₂ cups dried apricots

1¹/₂ cups pitted dates

1 tablespoon lemon juice

3 cups water

3/4 cup butter or oil

2 cups maple syrup

1 teaspoon vanilla

1 teaspoon cinnamon

6 cups pastry flour

2 teaspoons baking powder

2¹/₂ cups oats

These dense bars will please dessert lovers of all stripes. They are moist and cakey, and the apricot–date puree is both rich and light, offering a satisfying treat that won't make your teeth ache.

Preheat the oven to 350 degrees and grease a 9×13-inch pan.

In a large saucepan, combine the apricots, dates, lemon juice, and water. Bring the mixture to a boil over medium heat, then reduce the heat to low and simmer until the water is absorbed, about 20 minutes. Set aside to cool.

In a large bowl, combine the butter, maple syrup, vanilla, and cinnamon. In another bowl, mix the flour, baking powder, and oats. Add the flour mixture to the butter mixture and blend well. When the apricot mixture is cooled, puree it in a food processor until it is very smooth and spreadable. Spread two-thirds of the dough evenly over the bottom of the prepared pan. Then spread the apricot mixture evenly over the dough. Use the remaining dough to make a patchwork covering over the apricot layer. The top layer of dough doesn't need to cover every inch of the apricot, but distribute it evenly. Bake for 15 to 20 minutes.

THE FAMILY KITCHEN

This recipe requires creating a patchwork of dough on top of the apricot–date puree. You can teach kids the technique of moistening your hands with water so the dough doesn't stick and then let them design the top layer. Whatever it looks like before baking, it comes out looking beautiful.

Almond Joy Bars *

SERVES 18 TO 24

½ cup butter or oil, plus
2 tablespoons for glaze (use
oil for vegan version)

2 cups finely ground almonds

2½ cups maple syrup or
1¼ cups maple syrup
and 1¼ cups sugar

1 tablespoon almond extract

3 cups pastry flour

2 teaspoons baking soda

1½ cups shredded coconut

2 cups chocolate chips (check
that the chocolate does not
have added whey, milk fat, or
casein for vegan version)

These bars are inspired by (and obviously named for) the candy bar of my youth. The funny thing is, as a kid I never ate these candy bars. I was unaware of the joys of combining coconut, almonds, and chocolate. Fortunately for everyone, the combo has now made its way into my heart and this recipe (not to mention my stomach).

Preheat the oven to 350 degrees and grease a 7×11-inch pan.

In a bowl, beat the butter, almonds, maple syrup, and almond extract. In another bowl, mix the flour and baking soda. Add the flour mixture to the wet dough. Blend in the coconut and 1½ cups of the chocolate chips. The dough should be moist but thick enough to spread. Spread the dough evenly in the prepared pan. Bake until lightly browned but still very moist, about 15 minutes.

While the bars are cooling, melt the remaining ½ cup of chocolate chips with 2 tablespoons of butter or oil. Drizzle the glaze over the bars. Chill the bars until the topping is firm. For a fun alternative, use toasted hazelnuts instead of almonds.

THE FAMILY KITCHEN

The most fun part of this recipe is drizzling the melted chocolate on top. It does not really matter whether the chocolate is even or symmetrical, as long as it is reasonably well distributed.

Cashew Chocolate Brownies ⚘

BARS:

2 cups cashew butter

1/2 cup butter or oil (use oil for vegan version)

3 cups maple syrup or 1 1/2 cups maple syrup and 1 1/2 cups brown sugar

1 tablespoon vanilla

4 cups pastry flour

1 cup unsweetened cocoa powder

2 teaspoons baking soda

TOPPING:

1 cup cashew butter

3/4 cup maple syrup

1 tablespoon arrowroot

Nuts are the star in this recipe, which provides a great way to use homemade cashew butter (or another nut butter, if desired). In any case, these brownies, while decadent, are not too heavy to have two.

Preheat the oven to 350 degrees and grease a 7×11-inch pan.

Cream the nut butter, butter, maple syrup, and vanilla in a large bowl. In another bowl, stir together the flour, cocoa powder, and baking soda. Add the flour mixture to the butter mixture and blend well. Spread the dough into the prepared pan and bake for about 15 minutes.

While the bars bake, make the topping. Beat together the cashew butter, maple syrup, and arrowroot until the topping is smooth and easy to spread. When the brownies are cool, spread the topping over them and chill until cooled through.

ONE WAY TO INCREASE THE CHANCE OF SUCCESS FOR LOCAL WINERIES AND BREWERIES IS TO INCREASE THE DEMAND FOR THEIR FINE PRODUCTS, SO PAY ATTENTION TO THE SOURCE OF THE WINE AND BEER SERVED AT LOCAL RESTAURANTS AND SUPPORT THOSE CREATED WITH CARE NOT TOO FAR FROM YOUR HOME.

Green Beer
and Local Wine

BEER AND WINE ADD TO THE
ENJOYMENT OF EATING GREAT FOOD.
AS YOU DISCOVER AND ENJOY MORE
WAYS TO KEEP YOUR COOKING LOCAL,
YOU WILL FIND THAT YOU CAN APPLY
THE SAME PRINCIPLES TO YOUR
SELECTION OF BEER AND WINE.

In other words, "green beer" doesn't refer to the tap beer colored with green food coloring served in some pubs on St. Patrick's Day, but rather to beer (and wine) made locally and with sustainable growing methods.

As you engage in more local food practices, it will become increasingly clear that you are returning to the ways in which we lived, ate, and drank decades ago. Every community had its local brewery (which often also produced root beer or orange soda for the kids). Even in the Midwest, with its challenging winters, a number of wineries supplied juicy vintages throughout the late 1800s and early 1900s—until Prohibition killed this (ahem) fermenting industry.

Today, it is becoming easier and tastier to be green with your beer and wine purchases. Cold-hardy grape varietals are coming into their own, thanks to the dedication of grape growers such as the late Elmer Swenson, who devoted decades to growing grapes and offered the results of his self-directed and independent research to hundreds of growers and the viticulture program at the University of Minnesota. In the mid-1980s the university initiated a breeding program for wine grapes, directed by Peter Hemstad, and in 2000 the university completed a state-of-the-art enology laboratory and research winery. Today it is recognized as having one of the top wine-grape breeding programs in the United States. Four of the grape varieties (Frontenac, Frontenac Gris, Marquette, and La Crescent) are used to create excellent wines.

These new hybrid vines can withstand temperatures as low as minus 32 degrees Fahrenheit without freezing or splitting. An increasing number of Midwest winemakers are finding that in addition to being hardy, these grapes can make wines that stand on their own and in time could well attract the attention of boutique winemakers in the Big Three (California, Oregon, and Washington). Several Minnesota wineries are producing wonderful wines: the award-winning St. Croix Vineyards and Northern Vineyards of Stillwater, WineHaven Winery and Vineyard of Chisago City, Fieldstone Vineyards near Redwood Falls, and Morgan Creek Vineyards near New Ulm.

Weather is a much less a factor in producing a good brew. Good beer needs good grain, and some of the best grain in the world is grown in the Midwest—why else would vast tons of wheat from the Dakotas be exported to Italy for pasta making? Allegiance to a local brewery is a long-standing tradition, and loyalties will likely be sorely tested as the number of local and craft breweries increases.

The considerations that go into choosing locally produced beer and wine are the same as those for purchasing locally produced foods. As you choose which liquid bread or fruit of the vine to drink:

- **Look for local sources and producers**. Most local wineries, breweries, and locally owned wine and beer shops have online sites with lots of information about viticulture, brewing, and fermentation techniques and methods. The wines and beers are also described, so you can start to decide what you want to try.
- **With wine, look for cold-hardy varietals**. You might also find wines including Maréchal Foch or Seyval blanc, which are French–American hybrids. But if you learn that Cabernet Franc, Chardonnay, and Mourvèdre grapes are used in the wine, then it is likely the winemaker is buying grapes or juice from another grower outside the Midwest. These varietals belong to the *Vitis vinifera* species, and few, if any, are grown in Midwest vineyards. These grapes just cannot handle harsh winters without the grower having to bury each vine for the winter; that would get old within a few years and wreaks havoc with an already narrow profit margin. An adage states that the vines must suffer to produce good wine grapes, but that shouldn't mean that the grower needs to take on more than the already-substantial labor required to grow vines better matched to local weather conditions.
- When you're looking for a local wine that might become your own preferred house offering, **watch for varieties distinctively suited to the region**. Beyond the native American Concord and Catawba grapes, which conjure images of the supersweet and fortified syrups from Manischewitz and Mogen David, you will see French–American hybrids such as Baltica, Chancellor, Cayuga White, Chambourcin, Chardonel, Maréchal Foch, Landot noir, Norton, St. Vincent, Seyval, Seyval blanc, Traminette, Vidal blanc, Vignoles, and Zilga. Others to keep an eye out for include the godchildren of Elmer Swenson and varieties developed through the University of Minnesota: Alpenglow, Brianna, Edelweiss, Frontenac and its mutation Frontenac Gris, La Crescent, LaCrosse, Louise Swenson, Marquette, Prairie Star, Sabrevois, St. Croix, St. Pepin, Swenson Red, and Swenson White.
- If you do not live close to a winery or brewery, then **choose wine and beer that did not travel far to get to you**. One of the best and most enjoyable ways to discover these local producers of liquid refreshment is at your locally owned wine and beer shop. As you talk with the owner or salesperson, be open to suggestions and trust your own preferences. Like preferences in art, taste preferences in wine and beer are ultimately subjective. Pursue what you enjoy and what brings interest and pleasure to your table.
- In addition to appellation factors, **look for wine produced from grapes grown with eco-friendly methods**. Again, the best way to find these is to ask the crafter or shopkeeper. You can expect to find an increasing number of choices as producers move toward growing methods that rely less on fossil fuels and chemicals and more on solar, wind, and other sustainable practices.

One way to increase the chance of success for local wineries and breweries is to increase the demand for their fine products, so pay attention to the source of the wine and beer served at local restaurants and support those created with care not too far from your home. When you travel, you can support that area's local viticulture by choosing wine and beer from smaller boutique sources. These folks don't produce at levels that supply a large net of distribution, so if you find a small gem to your liking, purchase what you can pack or carry instead of adding to fossil fuel–intensive shipping methods.

You will feel a greater degree of satisfaction when you crack open a cold one bottled in a brewery a few blocks from your home or when you uncork a bottle of Seyval blanc made from grapes grown close to the banks of the Minnesota River. Adding products from artisanal and boutique wineries will enrich the degree to which you enjoy local food and bring you even deeper understanding of the meaning of *terroir*, or "taste of the earth."

SEASONAL MENUS WITH WINE RECOMMENDATIONS

AUTUMN DINNER

Roasted Garlic–Tomato Sauce with pasta (page 22)
Greens with Balsamic Vinaigrette (page 21)
Roasted Roots (page 59)

Wine pairing: A drier Frontenac rosé would hold up to the vinaigrette and the tomato sauce. A Marquette would complement the earthier flavors of the roasted roots and the sauce of the pasta course.

AUTUMN LUNCHEON

Stuffed Grape Leaves (page 4)
Luscious Lima Bean Salad (page 61)
Garlic–Almond Kale (page 58)

Wine pairing: To bring out the best of the fresh flavors of this Mediterranean menu, chill and serve a Frontenac Gris, which offers a soft spice, or a Seyval, a semidry white with a clean finish.

WINTER EVENING WARMING MEAL

Sun-Dried Tomato Pâté (page 5) served with Herbed Crackers
(page 145) and Wild Rice Crackers (page 146)

Hearty Black Bean Soup (page 43)

Latin "Couscous" (page 72)

Wine pairing: A red table wine with Frontenac or St. Croix
would complement the cumin in the soup without overpowering
the fresher flavors in the couscous.

||||||||||||||||||||||||||||||||||||||||||||||||||||||||||||||||||||||||||||||||||||||||||

WINTER BRUNCH

Turkey and Sheep-Cheese Quiche (page 110)

Roasted-Squash Gratin with Cilantro Pesto (page 103)

Banana–Cranberry Muffins (page 140)

Wine pairing: An off-dry Frontenac Gris is a nice contrast to the quiche
and would complement the squash and cilantro flavors. It can even work
pretty well with the banana notes in the muffins.

SPRING PICNIC

Savory Chard and Goat Cheese Tart (page 122)

Asparagus with Citrus and Olive Marinade (page 77)

Wine pairing: The floral notes of an off-dry La Crescent contrast well with the herbs and have an acidity that will cut through the goat cheese nicely. La Crescent can handle the challenge of asparagus and citrus.

||||||||||||||||||||||||||||||||||||||||||||||||||||||||||||||||||||||||||||||||||||||||||||||||

SPRING DINNER

Pizza with Arugula, Potatoes, Caramelized Spring Onions, and Gouda or Gorgonzola (page 114)

Early Greens with Miso Dressing and Toasted Almonds (page 78)

Wine pairing: Choose a wine with the properties of La Crescent, which can hold its flavor against the bite of the arugula and goat cheese.

SUMMER BRUNCH

Blackberry–Coconut Scones (page 144)

Falafel (page 127)

Cold Cucumber–Yogurt Soup (page 52)

Wine pairing: For this meal, you might opt instead for a proper tea,
iced or hot, but you could try a sweeter Edelweiss.

|||||||||||||||||||||||||||||||||||||||||||||||||||||||||||||||||||||||||||||||||||||||||||||||||||||||||||||

SUMMER GRILLING DINNER

Simple Garlic-Rubbed Salmon and Vegetables with
Sweet Basil Dressing (page 130)

Grilled Chicken with Barbeque Sauce (page 34)

Grilled Polenta with Three-Pepper Salsa (page 19)

Quinoa and Cucumber Salad (page 83)

Marinated Veggies (page 80)

Wine pairing: Bring out a hearty wine such as a Marquette, which will
work beautifully with the salmon and the chicken.

Acknowledgments

THE WRITING OF THIS BOOK HAS BEEN A LONG, ROUNDABOUT, AND COLLECTIVE CULINARY JOURNEY.

We are lucky to have the support of amazing friends, family, and partners who always believed in the Good Life and have been important to the creation of this book: Jenny's business partner and friend, Karn Anderson, who shared with her a vision that blossomed into a lifetime of shared food adventures; Jenny's husband and partner, Jon Dicus, who willingly tasted everything she ever prepared and always offered honest feedback; their daughters, Solana and Frances, who didn't exist when Jenny started this book but can now talk food and cooking with the best of them; her mother, Aviva, and siblings, who always supported her vision; Susan's children, Madeleine and Samuel Thurston Hamerski, who were willing tasters and cookbook commentators; Michael Hamerski, for making it easier to carve out time for working on the manuscript; Jenny's local food-writer inspiration, Beth Dooley, who is ebullient with praise and a fantastic chef; to the important women of the local foods movement who are driven by passion, know how to get things done, and make great food—Lucia Watson, Brenda Langton, and Tracy Singleton; the farmers and producers (including Greg Reynolds, Steven Read, Jodi Ohlsen Read, and Pam Benike) who were generous with their knowledge about sustainability and collaboration and work incredibly hard to produce the finest of real food; Tim Kenny at the University of Minnesota Landscape Arboretum for his wisdom, enthusiasm, and accurate eye; Peter Hemstad, University of Minnesota, and Anna Katharine Mansfield, Cornell University, for wise words about the vine and wine; Chris Halvorson, Neal Karlen, JoAnne Makela, Bridget Murphy, and Kit Naylor for their keen reading and comments; the writing women of Penchant and colleagues at the University of Minnesota for their unending encouragement for Susan's writing projects; Todd Orjala, editor of amazing and impeccable good taste; Kristian Tvedten, whose editorial assistance made the process a joy instead of a frustration; Pam Price, copy editor of insight and precision; and to everyone at the University of Minnesota Press for believing there is always room for more good, wholesome food.

Index

Gorgonzola

on pizza, 114

in potato gratin, 86

Gouda

on pizza, 114

in salad, 62, 69

Grains

cooking, 48

in croquettes, 107

in salad, 62, 69

See also specific grains

Granola, 147

Grape Leaves, Stuffed, 4

Gratin

with potatoes and gorgonzola, 86

with potatoes and tomato sauce, 131

with squash, 103

with winter vegetables, 113

Greek Squash or Pumpkin in Phyllo Casserole, 108–9

Green beans

in casserole, 135

gingered, 82

in salad, 129

Greens

in curry, 112

with pasta, 94

in salad, 57, 58, 78, 83, 85, 129

in soup, 50

Grilled Polenta with Three-Pepper Salsa, 19

Grilled salmon, 130

Grilled seafood, 136

Grilled vegetables, 24

"Growing Green Flavor," 64–65

Harvest Lasagna, 89–90

Harvest Medley, 40

Hearty Black Bean Soup, 43

Heirloom Tomato Sauce, 131

Herbed Crackers, 145

Herbed Yam and Potato Salad, 71

Herbs

in dumplings, 41

growing, 64–65

in salad, 63

Honey–Horseradish Sauce, 73

Israeli Couscous, 79

Italian Potato Soup, 37

Jam with polenta, 3

Kale

in casseroles, 124

in salad, 58

Kebabs, seafood, 136

Lasagna and lasagna sauce, 89–90

Latin "Couscous," 72

Layered Ginger Curry, 124

Leeks

in gratin, 86

in "risotto," 116

in salad, 57, 61, 69, 73, 79, 85

in sauce, 29

in soup, 39, 49, 52

in succotash, 99

Legumes

cooking, 7

in pâté, 6

See also Beans; Peanut(s)

Lemon–Poppy Seed Muffins, 141

Lemon–Poppy Seed Scones, 143

Lemons

flavor in sauces, 24, 25

in muffins, 141

Jenny Breen *(left)* has been cooking and baking professionally in the Twin Cities for more than twenty years. She is a co-owner of Good Life Catering (previously Good Life Café) and is a passionate advocate for local and sustainably raised foods. She received a Bush Leadership fellowship in 2009 and returned to school to study public health nutrition and continue her pursuit of healthy food for healthy families in healthy communities on a healthy planet. When not biking or canoeing with her family, she is in her home laboratory, passing along the pleasures of food to her husband, Jon, and their daughters, Solana and Frances.

Susan Thurston grew up on a farm in south central Minnesota, where her mother and grandmother taught her how to garden and cook with gusto. A poet, novelist, and journalist, she met Jenny Breen in her work with continuing education at the University of Minnesota. Her daughter, Madeleine, loves almost everything Susan cooks and writes; her son, Samuel, often thinks both are improved with a little butter and salt.